500 of the
Coolest Sites
for Cyberkids

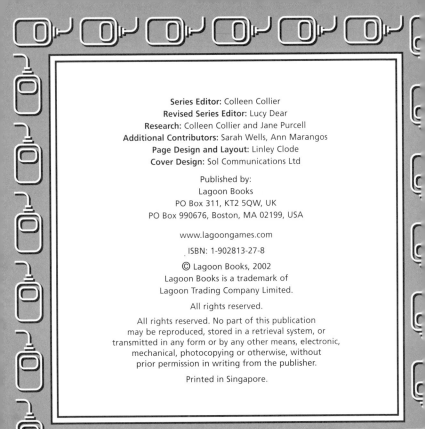

Series Editor: Colleen Collier
Revised Series Editor: Lucy Dear
Research: Colleen Collier and Jane Purcell
Additional Contributors: Sarah Wells, Ann Marangos
Page Design and Layout: Linley Clode
Cover Design: Sol Communications Ltd

Published by:
Lagoon Books
PO Box 311, KT2 5QW, UK
PO Box 990676, Boston, MA 02199, USA

www.lagoongames.com

ISBN: 1-902813-27-8

© Lagoon Books, 2002
Lagoon Books is a trademark of
Lagoon Trading Company Limited.

Printed in Singapore.

500 of the
Coolest Sites
for Cyberkids

LAGOON
BOOKS

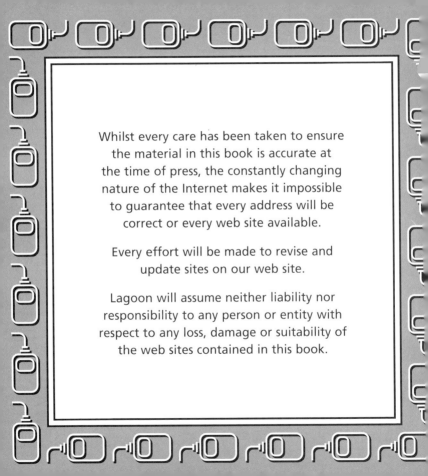

CONTENTS

INTRODUCTION

**'The Internet is a tidal wave…drowning those who
don't learn to swim in its waves' – Bill Gates**

Over the past few years, many guides to the Internet
have been written explaining how to access the Net
and how to use it. But now everyone's looking for a
fun and easy-to-use guide to the best sites, so here it is!

This stunning 288-page directory lists 500 of the Coolest
web sites around especially aimed at kids of all ages,
and is subdivided into six amazing chapters, according
to subject, to make searching even easier!

The research has been carried out by an avid team
of fun-loving Internet surfers (using a NetNanny
so nothing inappropriate is included), whose
brief was to find the funniest and most original sites
for kids to enjoy – which is just what they did!
Go to p220 or p229 to see what I mean!

1

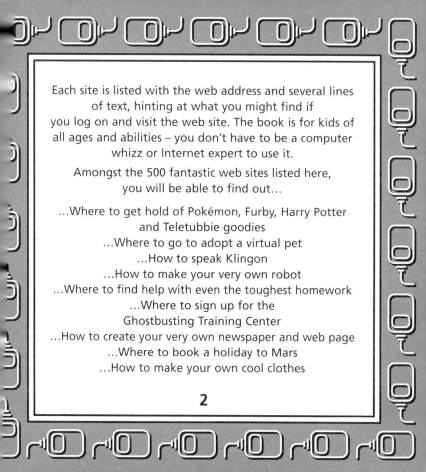

Each site is listed with the web address and several lines of text, hinting at what you might find if you log on and visit the web site. The book is for kids of all ages and abilities – you don't have to be a computer whizz or Internet expert to use it.

Amongst the 500 fantastic web sites listed here, you will be able to find out…

…Where to get hold of Pokémon, Furby, Harry Potter and Teletubbie goodies
…Where to go to adopt a virtual pet
…How to speak Klingon
…How to make your very own robot
…Where to find help with even the toughest homework
…Where to sign up for the Ghostbusting Training Center
…How to create your very own newspaper and web page
…Where to book a holiday to Mars
…How to make your own cool clothes

It's amazing what people put on the Internet, so here is the ultimate guide to finding all that is fun, fascinating, astounding and awesome!

Get online for hours of fun and entertainment!

If it's cool and especially for kids, you'll find it here!

3

1

Entertainment

Harry Potter Land
http://harrypotter.warnerbros.com/
Everything you need to know about the young hero of wizardry, Hogwarts and all. Read about his adventures and catch up on the latest info about the boy genius.

Movie Reporter
http://www.dove.org/
MovieReporter/dovereviews.htm
Want to know if the latest movies are hot or not? Well here are the latest reviews on all your favorites including 'Jurassic Park III' and 'Shrek'.

Pokémon Giggles!
http://www.kidsdomain.com/kids/pokeman/index/html

What Pokémon do you plant to grow a dinosaur? Answer – a Bulbasaur! If you get this, then you'll have a ball on the Pokémon web site.

Bookworm Bunch
http://www.pbs.org/bookwormbunch

Join Elliot Moose, Corduroy and the rest of 'The Bookworm Bunch' for secret facts, games, and show info.

Animorphs
http://scholastic.com/Animorphs

This site charts the futuristic adventure stories of young people who fight evil by morphing into animals…think of Power Rangers with fur and big teeth!

Wacky Web Tales
http://www.eduplace.com/tales

Choose from a list of story titles like 'Burp!' and 'Goaaal!' Fill in the form with your own words. Then sit back and giggle as your words are used to fill in the blanks to create a story of serious strangeness.

Garfield's Great
http://www.garfield.com

He's a crazy, lovable, orange cat and this is his site, jam-packed with book reviews, comics, fun and games. You can even email him and read the 'Garfield Gazette' newspaper.

Cool Cheapo Books
http://www.just-for-kids.com/

Thousands of books for and about kids all at discount prices. You can read reviews on the latest book releases before pestering your parents to buy them for you.

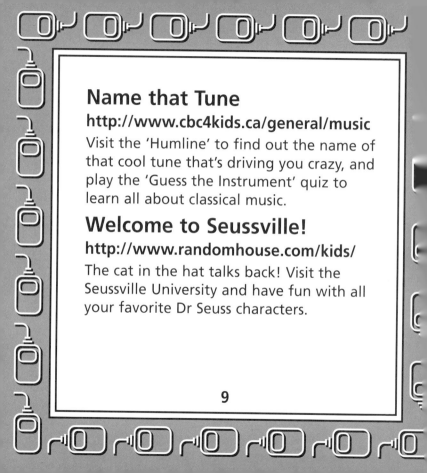

Name that Tune
http://www.cbc4kids.ca/general/music
Visit the 'Humline' to find out the name of
that cool tune that's driving you crazy, and
play the 'Guess the Instrument' quiz to
learn all about classical music.

Welcome to Seussville!
http://www.randomhouse.com/kids/
The cat in the hat talks back! Visit the
Seussville University and have fun with all
your favorite Dr Seuss characters.

Wired for Sound
http://www.niehs.nih.gov/kids/music.htm

Simply select a song from well over 100 in the 'Children's' list link, plug in your headphones, and listen to your favorites in super stereo.

10

Storybooks Online

http://www.magickeys.com/books

Award-winning site with original stories
(illustrated in great color), riddles, mazes
and coloring books.

Teenz Rule!

**http://www.cyberteens.com/
ctmain.html**

Billed as the Internet's Number One online
community for the world's youth, this site
features art and stories – you can even
submit your own work. Or write to Lola,
the advice columnist!

ABC Kids
http://www.eint.com/abagain/index.htm

Visit this site to meet Alaskan wolves, giggle at the jokes and visit Storyland, a special story site where you can take part in interactive games designed by kids.

Pickleberry Pie
http://www.childrensmusic.org

Want to listen to a radio show just for kids or join the wacky 'Rug Bugs' for 'Adventures on a Rug'? Then log on here and also download free music.

Cyberpigs
http://www.media-awareness.ca/ eng/med/kids/kindex.htm

If you're aged between 7 and 13, you'll love having adventures with the Cyberpigs, as well as finding out all about how TV, film, and video games are produced.

Disney Magic
http://www.disney.co.uk/DisneyOnline

Visit your favorite Disney cartoon characters at this funky site and find fun coloring books, wallpaper, and cool 'd' cards to send to all your friends.

Fun City
**http://www.motts.com/
kids/fun/color7.htm**

A coloring book web site for cybertots.
You can also make your own cards and
color them in. Lots of fun for budding
Picassos and you don't have to clear up the
mess afterwards!

A Girl's World
http://www.agirlsworld.com/

This is where girls rule the web, so check
out the things to try, make and do,
including decorating your jeans and
sneaking a peek at other girls' diaries.

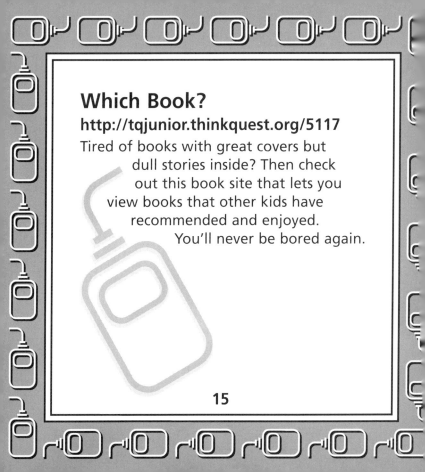

Which Book?
http://tqjunior.thinkquest.org/5117
Tired of books with great covers but dull stories inside? Then check out this book site that lets you view books that other kids have recommended and enjoyed. You'll never be bored again.

Fisher Price Fun Page
http://www.fisherprice.com/ us/fun/default.asp

Games and activities featuring stories from 'The Little People' toy range. Check out the personalized awards from the 'Rescue Heroes'.

Boys' Quest
http://www.boysquest.com

Learn how to make a solar-powered pocket watch, how to write a computer program, and discover some fun knot-tying tricks at this ezine that separates the men from the boys.

Gameboy Color
http://www.nintendo.com/

The home of finger-frenzy for game boys and girls. Gasp at the latest heartpumping adventures, plus previews of the hottest new games on the market.

Could You Be a Writer?
http://www.realkids.com

Think you're a budding author? This site is bursting with tips and advice and there's even a (gulp!) 'Writers' Critique Group' where your masterpiece will be read and commented on by other budding scribblers!

Just Write
http://www.justwrite.org

Does the next 'Booker Prize' have your name on it? Start scribbling your poems and stories now and then submit them here for other kids to read and enjoy.

Games Galore
http://www.irwintoy.com/ MicroSite/default.asp

Click on your favorite toy to reveal a world of fun, games, and news. If you're feeling kinda crafty, join the Beadalicious Babes, or step on the gas for fun with the Blazin' Key Cars.

18

American Girl
http://www.americangirl.com
Regularly updated, this site is full of different things to do every day, including making an enchanted garden, ideas for making cash, and tip-top tips.

Kids' Newsroom
http://www.kidsnewsroom.com
Impress your friends and be the first to know the latest music, entertainment and sports news before anyone else. There are games and quizzes too!

Barbie Land!
http://www.barbie.com/

The official web site for the grooviest
girl-doll around. Check out the
Barbie history section – you can
see how she was originally designed
to look back in 1959 and
follow her year-by-year
through some bad
hair days and serious
fashion disasters!

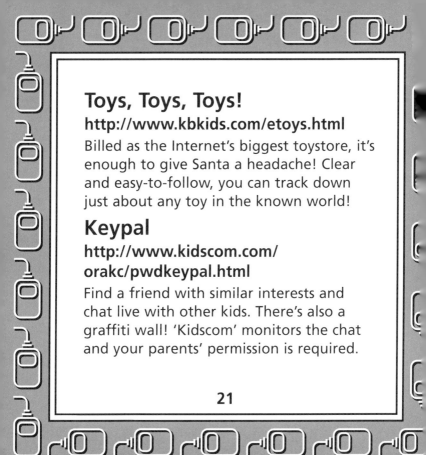

Toys, Toys, Toys!
http://www.kbkids.com/etoys.html
Billed as the Internet's biggest toystore, it's enough to give Santa a headache! Clear and easy-to-follow, you can track down just about any toy in the known world!

Keypal
http://www.kidscom.com/ orakc/pwdkeypal.html
Find a friend with similar interests and chat live with other kids. There's also a graffiti wall! 'Kidscom' monitors the chat and your parents' permission is required.

Purr-fect for Kids

http://www.purrfectforkids.com/

Believe it or not, learning can be fun! Check out the great toys and games at this site. They are fun and will help you use your noodle too!

'Lego' Action

http://www.lego.com/

Others may come and go but 'Lego' is still one of the most popular toys there is. You have to register to join the club but once you're in, there's a huge choice of 'Lego' games to play.

Oldies but Goodies!
http://www.got2haveit.com/

If you happen to be looking for an alien toy with a nine-inch head to make your collection complete, then this is the site for you!

Pokémon-sters
**http://www.pokemonsters
-toys-games.com**

This is really an online catalog dedicated to those little Japanese critters that are taking over the world. Be crafty and check out the plush toys with your parents just before your birthday!

Dr Toy
http://www.drtoy.com

There are thousands of award-winning toys here, all chosen by the good Dr Toy. Playing is good for your health – the doctor says so!

Warner Brothers Kids' Page
http://www.kids.warnerbros.com/

A one-stop site for all your favorite cartoon characters. Visit all the 'Looney Toons' characters, watch video clips and even learn how cartoons are made! You'll also find games, sounds and a coloring book.

24

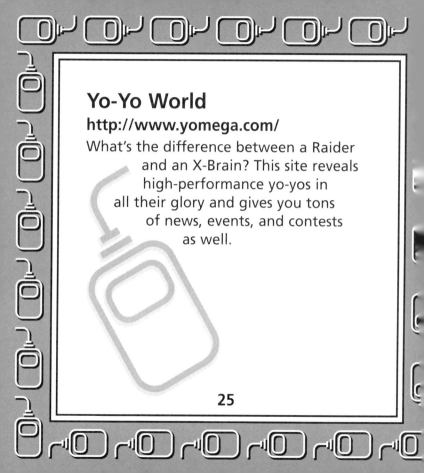

Yo-Yo World
http://www.yomega.com/
What's the difference between a Raider
and an X-Brain? This site reveals
high-performance yo-yos in
all their glory and gives you tons
of news, events, and contests
as well.

25

Huh?
**http://www.people.cornell.edu/
pages/jad22**

Click the 'Story Time' link to discover the
first lines of books that you must try to
guess the titles of. Go on smarty-pants, bet
you can't get them – it's not as easy as it
looks!

Yakityyak
http://www.yakityyak.com

Meet Purrscilla Cat, John Pig and the rest
of The Yak Pack, and then create gooey
recipes, read movie reviews, and learn fun
factoids.

Tons of Fun
**http://alfy.lycos.com/cool_sites/
Entertainment/Television_Cartoons.asp**

Get instant access to your favorite cartoon
characters, including 'Scooby Doo' and
'The Flintstones', and also enjoy games,
jokes, and puzzles that will guarantee
hours of fun!

Craft Cabin
**http://www.worldbook.com/
fun/wbla/camp/html/craft.html**

A great site if you like making your own
presents and toys. Mostly from stuff lying
around your house!

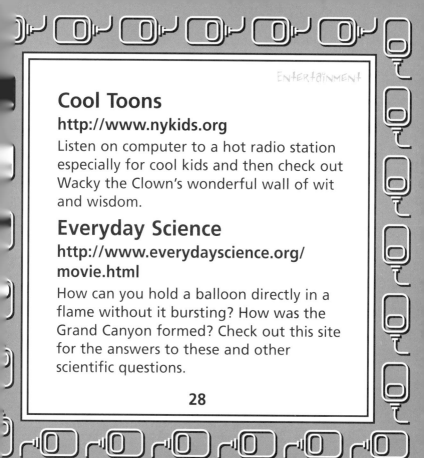

Cool Toons
http://www.nykids.org

Listen on computer to a hot radio station especially for cool kids and then check out Wacky the Clown's wonderful wall of wit and wisdom.

Everyday Science
http://www.everydayscience.org/movie.html

How can you hold a balloon directly in a flame without it bursting? How was the Grand Canyon formed? Check out this site for the answers to these and other scientific questions.

Hey Man – It's He-man!
http://www.toyarchive.com

Rare toys of the last 30 years can be found
at this interesting site. If you're after a
He-Man or a Jet Sled Two Pack, or maybe
some vintage 'Star Wars' merchandise, you
can send in pictures from your own archive
and swap information with other collectors.

Radio Hall of Fame
http://www.radiohof.org

Visit the Radio Hall of Fame and listen to,
and learn all about, the history of radio and
the people who helped shape it, including
the Lone Ranger and Groucho Marx.

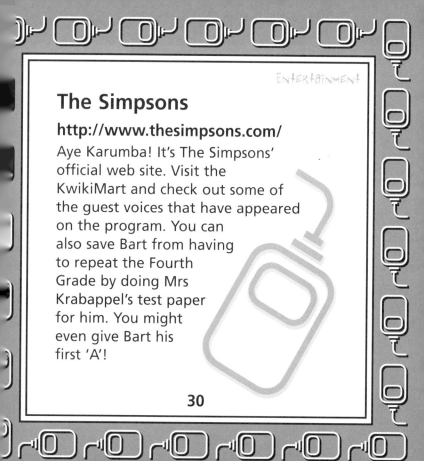

The Simpsons

http://www.thesimpsons.com/

Aye Karumba! It's The Simpsons' official web site. Visit the KwikiMart and check out some of the guest voices that have appeared on the program. You can also save Bart from having to repeat the Fourth Grade by doing Mrs Krabappel's test paper for him. You might even give Bart his first 'A'!

Nick Rules
http://www.nick.com
The home of your favorite TV network, here there is sport, music, blab and games, such as 'Agent Pixel' and 'Jimmy Neutron's Spaceblast 3D' game for you to enjoy.

Scooby Dooby Doo!
http://www.cartoonnetwork.co.uk/ index.html?section=microsites/scoobydoo
Find out what those pesky kids have got themselves into now!

Babe in the City
http://www.babeinthecity.com/
games/index.html

12 fun activities based on the porky movie
star. There are coloring books, mazes and
a piggy mobile to make.

Disney Jungle
http://disney.go.com/

This is where the magic lives online, so
click on the 'Fun Finder' button for
activities, games, painting and stories.

Celebrity Pics
http://www.yahooligans.com/
arts_and_entertainment/movies/
Actors_and_Actresses/

Loads of great sites off this one, filled with facts and info about your favorite movie stars!

Brady World
http://www.bradyworld.com/
sketch/castindx.htm

The cyberhome of the spookily perfect TV family from the '70s. Go to the opening page and click on the Brady you want to know about most.

Leo Is King!

http://www.leonardodicaprio.com/

The official site for all Leo-maniacs. You can download lots of pictures, check out his biography and find out what he's up to at the moment. There's also an online fan club for you to join.

Comic Capers

http://www.blackberrycreek.com/cbk

Vote for the best comics here made by kids for kids like you, and even have a go at being a comic creator yourself. You can also create comic cards and subscribe to the Blackberry Creek Newsletter.

Sticky and Icky
http://yucky.kids.discovery.com

Learn about your body, visit worm world and roach world, make revolting recipes and try icky experiments. You'll even discover why you burp!

Pokémon – The Movie

http://pokemonthemovie.warnerbros.com/

You can download Pokémon backgrounds from the movie and other goodies. There's a quiz where, if you answer all the questions right, it leads you to more Pokémon fun!

Keep on Dancing

http://library.thinkquest.org/J002266F

Think you have what it takes to be the next Michael Jackson or Britney Spears? Then check out the different types of dancing here and get ready to strut your stuff.

36

My Story's on TV!
http://www.storystudio.com/

If you've ever wanted to write for television, here's your chance. You can submit a story to this Canadian television show that dramatizes stories written by 10-14 year olds.

Foxy Kids!
http://www.foxfamilychannel.com/

Learn about the programs made on the Fox Family Network for children, such as 'The Wiggles', 'The Jellababies' or 'Angela Anaconda'. Or you could go to the game site and play games like 'Freakout Jam'.

TV Old and New
http://www.mztv.com/

Check out the gallery of funky old TV sets.
Marvel at the days when it was only in
black and white! Contribute to the oral
history of television by writing about how
much television means to you.

Fishy Film Footage!
http://www.footageworld.com

Check out the free downloads from
this massive film footage company and
watch fish swim across your screen.
The underwater footage is awesome!

Boogie at Club-E
http://www.athropolis.com/

If you love to sing and dance, then boogie on down to Sharon, Lois and Bram's Club-E. Lots of games and stories for you to get with the beat.

Kididdles
http://www.kididdles.com/

Go on a guided tour of the musical 'Mouseum' with MoJo, the all-singing, all-dancing mouse. If you're looking for a song, MoJo can help you through the Alpha Index. There's a Kididdles survey you can take part in too!

Want a Record Contract?
http://www.ajkids.com

Supposing you land yourself a record
contract at the age of nine?
What do you do? Ask Jeeves
of course! He knows everything!

Singing and Swinging
http://members.home.com/
veeceet/index.html

A site for budding crooners. There are popular nursery rhymes, just-for-fun songs, special Christmas and holiday songs and even a few folk tunes.

Global Gang
http://www.globalgang.org.uk

Join the Global Gang and find out about the lives of children in other parts of the world, as well as a ton of news, games, gossip and fun to keep you amused. It's out of this world!

41

Magic Kat
http://www.frontiernet.net/ ~jackson/magickat.htm

If you want to see Magic Kat pull a bear out of his hat, check out this fun animated magic show for kids of all ages.

Rock Me Amadeus!
http://www.w-a-mozart.com/

A cool site for the world's hottest musician…Mozart. Listen to some of the most beautiful music ever written!

Emma's Galaxy

http://members.dencity.com/emmasgalaxy/

Designed by ten-year-old Emily, this excellent site is both dedicated to her dog and a clever twist on 'Star Wars'. Check out 'Dog Wars', 'Death Dog Strikes Back' and 'Return of the Dog', complete with pictures!

The Noodlehead Network

http://www.noodlehead.com/

You'll love this site if you're a budding Steven Spielberg because it's full of great stuff about filming techniques.

Kids' Space
http://www.kids-space.org

Entertain yourself by visiting art galleries full of kids, drawings, read fun stories, talk to other kids in the chat room and even find a pen pal to write to.

Sesame Street
http://www.sesameworkshop.org

How do you get to Sesame Street? Why, you log on here for dragon tales, sticker world, and the passport kids, plus all your favorite TV characters.

Daddy-a-go-go!
http://www.daddyagogo.com/bio.html
Here is a whole web site of tunes that the whole family can suffer to. You can listen to such groovin' techno classics as 'Brush your Teeth', 'Ants in my Pants', and the ever-popular 'The Thang from Planet Twang'.

45

Musical Birthdays
http://DataDragon.com/day/select.shtml

Tap in your birthday and check out which famous people you share yours with, what Broadway show opened that day and, most importantly, who topped the charts!

Orchestral Maneuvers
http://datadragon.com/education/instruments/

This classical site provides a great way to find out about the different sections of an orchestra. Click on icons to hear instruments played!

Radio Fridge
http://www.montyharper.com/
CMW/Kids.html

Check out the Radio Refrigerator where
you can listen to a huge variety of music
and stories online. There's a message board
where you can make new friends too.

1990s' Knowledge
http://www.concentric.net/
~Pjreilly/the1990s.shtml

Are you a big fan of the '90s' film and
music scenes? Test your knowledge to see
how much you really know.

Magic Moments

http://www.conjuror.com/magictricks

Amaze and astound your parents and friends by learning the free tricks for new magicians at this marvelous site, including 'The Unbreakable Match' and 'The Magic Question Answering Pendulum'.

Got the Blues?

http://www.worldbook.com/ fun/aamusic/html/blues.htm

Learn about the roots of the Blues and the most influential Blues artists, from Ray Charles to BB King.

Peanuts Party
http://www.snoopy.com

This is the home of 'Peanuts' on the web and there are trivia quizzes, coloring books, cartoons and a 'Who's Who' of all the TV characters to keep you happy for hours.

Funkadelic
http://www.judyanddavid.com

Judy and David are two Juno award-winning stars of Canadian children's TV. You can tell that they know their stuff from this colorful and funky music site. There's an online songbook and lots of games!

2

Gadgets and Gizmos

Gizmo Magic

http://www.makegizmos.com/ projects.htm

Tons of hands-on fun at this great gizmo site. Before you know it, you too will be able to make a Hummer Buzzer and a Dragon Kite!

Dress Up

http://www.surfnetkids.com/ dressup.htm

Play interactive dress-up games. You can clothe Dinorella the dainty dinosaur for the ball, or dress up Dunstan the Chimp (from the movie 'Dunstan Checks In').

Gizmo Crafts
http://www.makestuff.com/kidstuff.html

There is a huge range of gizmos and gadgets for you to make here, including film cannister rockets and body tracing. It's fun, easy and cheap, so what are you waiting for?

Crafty Crafts
http://crafterscommunity.com/kids/

For smaller kids, there's tons of ideas for simple crafts here, and for older children there's masses of ideas for making your own clothes and accessories.

Aunty Beeb

http://www.bbc.co.uk/ gameskids/gadgets/gadgets.shtml

Get the latest gadgets and gossip here! The very latest gadgets are reviewed and there is also a whole range of games for you to play.

Fantasy T-Shirts

http://www.smallfaces.com

This creative T-shirt company had the neat idea of T-shirts decorated with the torso of a fantasy character and you provide the 'head'! There are over 30 great designs to choose from!

TV Toys
http://www.tvtoys.com

Although fun to play with, toys inspired by TV series are highly collectible too! If you are too young to remember 'Chips' and 'Mork and Mindy', log on here and remember, they may be old but soon they will be worth a fortune!

It's a Jungle!
http://jungle.com

Packed full of CDs, videos, computers, and games, this is a web site full of every dream gadget imaginable!

Kids' Gear

http://www.bgtk.ige.com/gadgets.htm

Whether you're a big kid or small fry, the latest gear can be seen here first. Check out the boomboxes and two-way radios!

Future Gadgets

http://cbc4kids.ca/general/time/ millennium/gadgets.html

What new gizmos will be essential to us in the not-too-distant future? Log on here to find out – there's everything from the Solo Trek Exo-Skeletor Flying Vehicle to buildings made of bubbles to choose between.

Gurl Pages
http://www.gurlpages.com

Yes, it's a web site for 'gurls' as opposed
to 'girlies'. There's loads to do,
including a celebrity adoration
page, a ranting and raving page,
strange obsessions, computer info,
and a very good fashion
section. Try out 'Jessica's
Fashion Philosophy' to
learn what's hot and
what's not in the
world of teen
fashion!

Cosmo Girl
http://www.cosmogirl.com/

Cosmo Girl is the baby sister of *Cosmopolitan* magazine. Tons of style, make-up and hair advice and you can also get in touch with your 'inner self'.

Spy Kids
http://www.spykids.com

Find out all about the movie that made kids into James Bond, on a mission to save the planet and their parents using amazing gadgets and gizmos along the way.

Adventure Kit
http://www.adventurekit.com

Hit the wilderness trail and check out the survival gadgets and gizmos at this site. There's everything you can imagine from photon micro-lights to V7 watches.

Lindzi's Page of Insanity
http://www.lindzi.com

Popular ezine run by real girl Lindzi. It's a bit like having a clued-up older sister on site who dispenses lots of hot-style tips and some good advice. You go, girl!

58

Models Online
http://www.models-online.com
If you really want to try your hand at the modeling business, then this global network will tell you what you need to know to get started.

Planet Supermodel
http://www.supermodel.com
Do not log onto this page if you are having a bad hair day. This site has everything you could possibly want to know about Planet Supermodel. There's advice and contacts for all would-be Naomis and Lindas.

Boys' Toys
http://www.big-boys-toys.net/acatalog/index.html

Think James Bond at this online store that has a huge range of electrical equipment, extreme sports equipment, and models and radio-controlled gadgets.

Fat Cat Inc.
http://www.fatcats.com

The home of the fashion-conscious feline – meet Mel and Chuck, cutout kitties, and check out the latest in 'cat fashion'. There's a Fat Cat of the Month, which features one dressed up in human clothes!

Dr Gadget
http://www.drgadget.co.uk
This is the home of top quality toys and gadgets for everyone aged 5 to 95! It includes hot air balloons, 3D hologram gadgets and flying blimps.

Boys in Dresses
http://members.tripod.com/ ~histclo/intro.html
Boys! If you had been born in the nineteenth century, you would probably be sporting a dress! This fab site looks at the 'development of boys clothes over the last 500 years'.

61

Kope's Gadgets

http://www.kopes.com/kids/index.htm

Check out the latest spy gear at Kope's
site, as well as the cool robots and solar
car kits. A good site to point your parents
to around Christmas!

Potato Power

**http://www.discoverymart.com/
gadgets.html**

The gadgets and gizmos here are fun to
play with as well as put on show. Have a
look at the 'Two Potato Clock', which is
powered by potatoes, and the funny
'Drinking Bird'.

Hammacher Schlemmer
http://www.hammacher.com/children/cindex.asp

Despite the funny name, this gadget store has a great kids range, including inflatable sleds, backyard ice rinks and kids bank tellers.

Baaad Fads
http://www.badfads.com

Did you know that bell-bottoms and sideburns were once the height of chic? Go ask your dad then, or else click onto the fashion section of the Bad Fads museum.

Cookscorner
http://www.cookscorner.com/shop

If you are a budding chef, you'll love all the fun kitchen gizmos here, including heart-shaped cookie cutters and cookie jars.

Funky Fabulous Fashion
http://www.fashionangel.com/

These 'fashion angels' trawl the web for current cool gear, second-hand bargains, alternative fashion and anything else you might need to get dressed in the morning.

Elle's Belles
http://www.elle.com/

Ezine version of the popular fashion
magazine. *Elle* is sold in over 12 countries
so it's truly international. You can make
your own cosmetics and join the Club Elle
community!

Don't Give Me Lip!
http://www.thelipstickpage.com

Fun guide to everything kissable! Shoot
off to the celebrity lipstick page to copy
what Kate Moss or Naomi Campbell are
wearing on their lips, or check out the
brilliant cosmetics' exchange network.

Stinky Trainer Site
http://sneaker-nation.com
Welcome to Planet Trainer, the site for everyone who feels naked without them. Swap ideas with other sneaker seekers on the message board or check out whether you're wearing 'Hot Trainers' or 'Not Trainers'.

Hot Shoe Shuffle
http://www.centuryinshoes.com
Yes, there were shoes before trainers! Check out this speedy musical sprint through a century of footwear. Be awed by a gallery of history's hottest shoes.

66

Face Facts

http://www.facefacts.com

The Face Facts home is 'packed wall-to-wall with acne information'. It's divided into rooms and each one has a specific function. Email a doctor from the privacy of the 'bedroom'; go to the 'kitchen' to check out the facts and myths surrounding greasy food; or look at pimple remedies in the 'bathroom'. All you have to do is pick a spot to start!

Cool Hobbies
**www.kidinfo.com/
Student_Leisure/Hobbies.html**

Go to a world of jewelry-making, knitting, beadwork and sewing. You could even learn to make your own soap and start an empire!

Space Magic
**http://www.thewritersedge.com/
gadgets.cfm**

Boldly go where others have gone before and check out these space-tastic gadgets developed by those clever people at NASA!

Boys – Dress to Impress!
http://www.manslife.com/
clothes/howtodress

This nifty style guide tells you everything you need to know about being a sharp dresser – don't get dressed without it!

Space Crafts
http://www.dltk-kids.com/
crafts/space/space.html

Using household items, you can learn to make cool space gizmos at this far-out site. Choose from a 'Moon Rock Craft' or a 'Universe in a Jar'.

The Beauty Channel
http://www.beauty-channel.com/index.html

Beautify your life! A really good-looking site – it's got tons of advice, goodies and how-tos from the experts.

Toy Frenzy
http://www.shoplifestyle.com/store/?source=goto

Fancy trying virtual snowboarding and virtual skateboarding? All the equipment to do it can be found here, as well as lightning speed flip-over dragsters and mini-accordions.

Zit Busters

http://www.whatshouldido.com/
acne/html

Hey kids, zits happen! This short site is a
fast reference guide to knowing when it's
just part of the teen terrain or time to go
to a doctor!

Fun for All

http://www.sharperimage.com

View the latest gizmos for all ages
including water-resistant CD players for
the shower and electric scooters and
walkie-talkies.

Goofy Inventions
http://www.totallyabsurd.com

Award-winning wacky site that looks at
the funniest inventions ever. The absurd
archive has hundreds of time-wasting
treasures, like the giant duck decoy, the
greenhouse biosphere helmet and the
kissing shield. You'll laugh out loud!

Going Cuckoo!
http://www.meddybemps.com

Come into the big house and meet Weebit
Cuckoo who makes wonderful clocks and
mechanical toys. You can play with them
and a wonderful interactive light display.

72

Gadget Mania

http://www.penguinputnam.com/yreaders/toybox

Click on the 'Young Readers' link and you can learn how to make hair wraps, corkscrews or a bracelet on this fun activity site for kids.

Got a Gizmo?

http://www.gadgets-gifts.com

Look for cool toys and gifts here that you can then pester your parents for, including wind-up radios and water-powered clocks.

Gadget Review
http://it.asia1.com.sg/ v2/reviews/gadgets.html

If it's new, it will be tested and reviewed here first. Be the first to know about the latest stuff before all your friends and before it hits the shops!

Girl-tech
http://www.girltech.com

Are you paranoid? Then check out these hilarious e-gadgets for total girl privacy – although there's no reason why boys couldn't use them too!

Virtual 'Titanic'

http://www.discovery.com/stories/science/sciencetitanic/sciencetitanic.html

Walk around the virtual 'Titanic' from the movie, and check out some of the treasure that was found after 70 years at the bottom of the sea. Awesome!

Personal Web Page

http://www.smplanet.com/webpage/webpage.htm

It's a lot simpler than it looks – in seven easy steps, this great site shows you everything you need to know about creating a web page.

75

RadGad
**http://www.radgad.com/
feature.html?CREF=372**

Visit this site for useful gadgets and
gizmos that'll blow your socks off,
including saucer shooters, virtual golf
games and inflatable swimming pools.

Cyber Cards
http://www.bluemountain.com

Forgotten a friend's birthday? Cyber
your way back into their good books by
sending a free personalized card. You can
add a voice message and an optional
personal message as well.

Cyberkids
http://www.cyberkids.com
There's plenty to do at this fun site
which includes an online shooting gallery.
It will even let you spell your name using
Egyptian hieroglyphics!

Monster Fights
http://www.jitterbug.com
Welcome to the site, O Fighting One.
Who will win the battle of the cyberpets?
Enter, steel yourself and find out.

Barking Mad
http://www.virtualdog.com/

If it's really a dog you're after, then
this virtual dog pound offers the
biggest selection of wet-nosed
hounds. Once you've picked and
named your pooch, learn about the
breed and give it a license.
Apart from being fun, this
is an excellent way to
really think about the
serious responsibility
of training, walking
and feeding a
real dog.

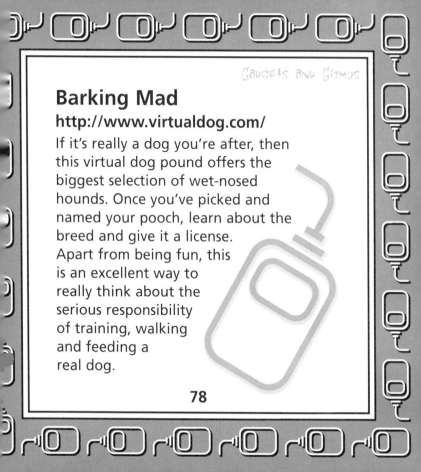

78

Virtual Pet Homepage
http://www.virtualpet.com/vp/

You can download and care for practically any pet, from a low-maintenance hamster or fish to the biggest dog you can find, at this site!

How Stuff Works
http://www.howstuffworks.com

If you've ever been awake at night wondering how planes fly, 'How Stuff Works' lives up to its name and explains how anything works.

Ask a Gadget Whizz

**http://www.newscientist.com/
lastword/topics/gadgets1.jsp**

This cool site has experts to answer all
your questions about gadgets. Post your
thorny questions on the message board or
have fun searching the archive!

HotWheels

**http://www.hotwheels.com/
kids/2001/index.asp**

Let's burn cyber rubber, baby! A site for
motoring maniacs, HotWheels gives you
the lowdown on the coolest cars around.

Funology
http://www.funology.com

This site features fun gadgets and gizmos such as lava lamps that you can learn to make, as well as a huge range of other fun craft projects for you to enjoy.

Build Your Own Rocket!
http://www.alaskascience.com

Come on, you've always wanted to! If you happen to have some scotch tape, thick paper and a plastic straw lying around, follow the six easy steps to rocket success. 'Houston we have a problem.'

Plant Parts
**http://www.hhmi.org/
coolscience/vegquiz/index.html**

Play the plant parts learning game online
and test your science knowledge at the
same time.

Paw Island
http://www.pawisland.com

Have a fantastic interactive adventure on
Paw Island with a whole host of fun
characters to guide you. You can enjoy the
day's giggletoon and other fab activities.

Feeling Spacy?
http://www.holodeck3.com

The 'Star Trek' Holodeck is known among Trekkies as one of the best sites on the Internet. Log on, choose the department you want to work in, and then..."Beam me up, Scotty"!

If It's a Gadget – We Have It!
http://www.gadgets-inc.com/

Recorders, telephones, scanners, surveillance equipment and other snooper-type things are available here!

Back-to-School
**http://www.usatoday.com/
life/cyber/ccarch/cckim050.htm**

This web site gives you the latest lowdown
on what cool gadgets are considered the
best for savvy students at school. There are
tons of cyber goodies for you to view and
drool over.

Extremely Useless
http://www.uselesstoys.com/

There's some totally indispensable stuff here
like a finger skateboard, huge laser pointers
and wrestling stickers. How have you
managed to live this long without them?

The Lone Zone
http://www.lonezone.com
The mission on this site is to 'check out the weirdest gadgets and bring them to your attention'. How about a pocket rocket massager? No, I don't know what it's for either!

Specs Appeal
http://www.rainbowsymphony.com/
See the world in a whole new way with these sassy 3D specs and groovy glasses. You can even custom-design your own pair! They won't improve your eyesight but they'll certainly get you noticed!

The Only Number You Need
http://www.roydburn.com/007/

Pay attention 007! Check out this 'shaken, not stirred' site for movie information, interviews, and the ultimate boy toys!

Dirt Devils
http://www.dirtkids.com/
page12novelty.htm

If you are into motorbike racing and gadgets, you'll love this site that is jam-packed full of gizmos and gadgets especially for bike fans everywhere!

The Stupid Zone
http://www.stupid.com/giftshop

A mobile phone that smells? You must be in the stupid zone! It's bursting with strange and silly gizmos. Check out the talking Austin Powers key ring and the 'Titanic' robot!

Weird Science
http://www.0-0-0checkmate.com/ DesignScienceToys/ Mini_Hoberman_Sphere

Be a science buff and check out the globe puzzles, magnetic toys and bugs – all with a scientific twist!

The Leftie Site

http://www.southpaw-pineapple.com

Are you left-handed? Be proud of it with left-handed T-shirts, mugs and school supplies that save you the strain of opening a book the wrong way!

Solar Robots

http://www.solarbotics.com

Welcome to Solarbotics, where robots are thought to be a big part of the future. Check out what Mark Tilden (the original BEAM Roboticist!) has created and what he thinks the future holds for us all.

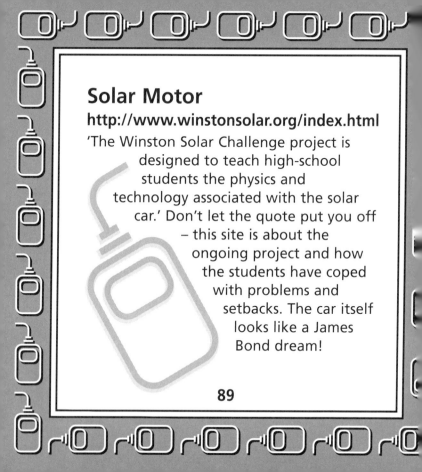

Solar Motor

http://www.winstonsolar.org/index.html

'The Winston Solar Challenge project is designed to teach high-school students the physics and technology associated with the solar car.' Don't let the quote put you off – this site is about the ongoing project and how the students have coped with problems and setbacks. The car itself looks like a James Bond dream!

Li'l Hands
http://www.lilhands.ca/products.html

If you have little hands and are tired of
everything being too big for you to hold,
you'll go nuts over the special gadgets and
gizmos that have been invented just for
you. You'll never have to struggle with
that full-size remote or mouse again!

Techno-Science!
http://www.popsci.com

Check out the latest gadgets in science,
technology and home entertainment. If it
is going to be big, this is where you'll see
it first.

90

Rocket Science
http://www.xfrresh.com

If it's new and cool, you'll find it at this wicked teen site that has everything from palmtops to phones.

Egg Gadgets
http://www.houseofhen.com/article1017.html

Egg gadgets – can you really live without them? Log on to this weird site to find out what they are.

I Want It!
http://www.iwantoneofthose.com
The address says it all! – here is the stuff
you want but don't necessarily need,
including the Astronaut Pen originally
issued by NASA in 1965!

Galaxy Gizmos
http://starwars.hasbro.com
In a galaxy far, far away, there is a site
that has a huge range of 'Star Wars'
gadgets, gizmos and toys waiting for you
to discover them. Log on now and be
transported to a world far away.

Metal Mickey
http://www.robotstore.com

Imagine having your own robot, programmed to do your bidding! Well, this fab site will provide you with a robot kit so you can put one together and never have to clean your room again!

Games Paradise
http://www.gamesparadise.com

Wonder where all the kids at school find out about the latest computer games? Chances are, it is at this fantastic site!

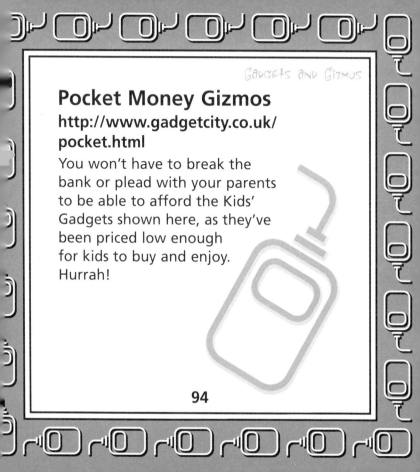

Pocket Money Gizmos
**http://www.gadgetcity.co.uk/
pocket.html**

You won't have to break the
bank or plead with your parents
to be able to afford the Kids'
Gadgets shown here, as they've
been priced low enough
for kids to buy and enjoy.
Hurrah!

Shop Smart
http://www.shopsmart.com

If you are determined to get the best at the lowest prices, check out this online store where you actually compare prices on all the latest goods and find a bargain!

One-stop Shop
http://www.funideas.com

The self-proclaimed 'one-stop shop for gags, gifts, jokes, novelty items, pranks, smells, and noises'. It's all here!

$$\frac{3}{Sport}$$

Major League Baseball

http://www.majorleaguebaseball.com

Visit this web site for cool pitching tips or find that baseball term you've forgotten. Packed with tips, information and major league links to other cool baseball sites.

Chicago Cubs Roar

http://www.cubs.mlb.com/ NASApp/mlb/chc/homepage/ chc_homepage.jsp

This is the official site of the Chicago Cubs, filled with the latest team news, events and headlines. There are even games in the kids' section for you to discover!

Karate Kids
http://www.blackbeltmag.com

Never mind fashion – get yourself a real black belt in this cool ezine for high-kicking kids. Great for the rookie Bruce Lee – it's packed with information on all the different types and levels of martial arts.

Ninja Nippers
http://www.winjutsu.com/ ninjakids/index.html

Never mind green teenage turtles, this is the real thing! Impress your friends with some simple Ninjutsu moves, practiced by the ancient masters.

Shotokan? Course You Can!
http://www.shotokanforeveryone.com

One of the newest types of martial arts –
it's only 100 years old! Master the kid
brother of karate with different types of
blocks and positions and find out where
you can learn for real.

Karate For U
http://www.ckfa.com/start.htm

Meet the kids at the cool-kicking Martial
Arts Academy for Kung Fu. Clock some
fabulous pictures of the grandfathers of
karate showing off their moves. Want to
be as fit as that when you're 60?

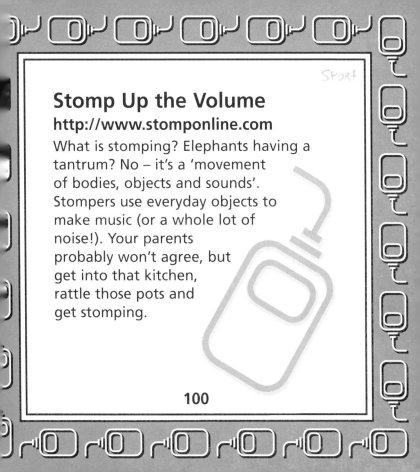

Stomp Up the Volume
http://www.stomponline.com

What is stomping? Elephants having a tantrum? No – it's a 'movement of bodies, objects and sounds'. Stompers use everyday objects to make music (or a whole lot of noise!). Your parents probably won't agree, but get into that kitchen, rattle those pots and get stomping.

100

B-Boing!

http://www.bboy.com

The home of online hip-hop, you can learn to bust a move, download music, and check out the gallery of pictures, graffiti, and flyers.

Run Around Sioux

http://www.powwows.com/dancing

Don't be a Sitting Bull. Learn how to pow-wow and try out some Native-American dances like 'The Buckskin Wiggle', 'The Fancy Feather' and 'The Jingle'.

Balti Blast
http://www.baltimoreblast.com
No, this isn't an Indian food snack site –
it's the Baltimore indoor soccer players!
You can contact the real team by email
and get some tips and advice.

Volleyball
http://www.volleyball.com
Hit the beach in style after you have
checked out this great volleyball site, filled
with info on where to play, what to play,
the pros, and advice in Coach's Corner.

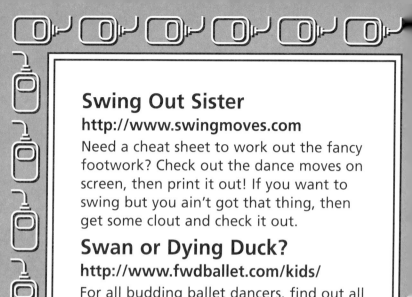

Swing Out Sister
http://www.swingmoves.com

Need a cheat sheet to work out the fancy footwork? Check out the dance moves on screen, then print it out! If you want to swing but you ain't got that thing, then get some clout and check it out.

Swan or Dying Duck?
http://www.fwdballet.com/kids/

For all budding ballet dancers, find out all you need to know about classical ballet for kids – where you can get lessons and pick up the lingo – soon you'll be able to tell your 'allegro' from your elbow!

Flaming Flamenco
http://www.flamenco-world.com

Get those maracas clacking with some hot Spanish flamenco. Check out the great pictures of gypsy dancers, and find out where you can learn to click more than just your mouse!

Riverdance
http://www.riverdance.com

Go backstage with the international Riverdance team. Who would have thought that putting your arms by your sides and jigging up and down could be so cool?

Cool Capoeira
http://www.capoeirasj.com

Get to grips with this funky Brazilian martial art. It's a mix of karate and dance, it's 400 years old and it's taking the world by storm! Take a lesson online and put a feather in your capoeira.

105

Checkered Flag
http://www.ddavid.com/formula1
Featuring the history, drivers and tracks, this is the ultimate Grand Prix web site for fans of burning rubber everywhere!

Scrum!
http://www.scrum.com
The latest in the world of rugby – all the games, player profiles and posters you could possibly want or need!

Electro Gym
http://www.gymn-forum.com

Need some gymnastic inspiration? This site has tons of pictures of the greatest gymnasts ever and some of their gravity-defying feats.

BetterBodz
http://www.betterbodz.com/kids.html

Learn all about the skeleton system that holds you together and the importance of muscles and how they work at this helpful sports site that also includes cool coloring books and other fun.

Aim & Fire
http://library.thinkquest.org/27344/heavy.htm

Known as the sport of champions, you can learn its history and how to play here. What are we talking about? – why, archery of course!

Which Sport?
http://library.thinkquest.org/J003198

Why are team sports great for kids like you? Find out here and also discover tons of info about different sports and how to play them.

Baywatchers
http://www.jrlifeguards.com
If you'd love to be a lifeguard, check out the cool Californian Junior Lifeguard site. Read all the mega safety tips and test your knowledge of the sea.

Scuba-doo, Where Are You?
http://www.scubadiving.com
If you want to hang out beneath the sea, then 'wet' your appetite with some awesome video footage of scuba divers.

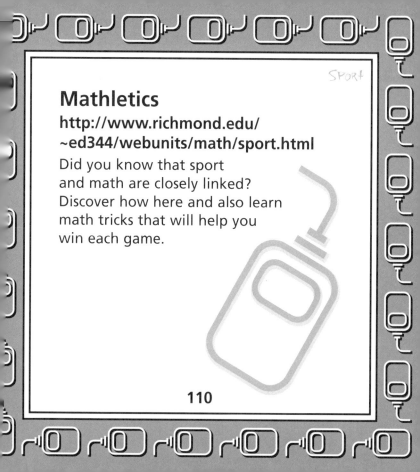

Mathletics
**http://www.richmond.edu/
~ed344/webunits/math/sport.html**

Did you know that sport
and math are closely linked?
Discover how here and also learn
math tricks that will help you
win each game.

Badminton Barmy
http://www.intbadfed.org/rules.html

Before you even lift a shuttlecock and start playing, you should check out this site and get great tips on how to play, all the rules, and the aim of the game.

Sore Toe
http://www.smartplay.net

Read sports star profiles and get great advice from sport celebs about playing safely and what to do if you get injured. Great FAQs and links as well!

Brain Muscles

http://www.iis-sports.com/trivia/

Give your brain a workout with this great sports quiz. It's updated every month so you can keep going back for more. Get the answers right and win a prize!

Fight Like Zorro!

http://www.britishfencing.com

Check out the moves and discover more about one of the world's oldest sports. You'll be cool, co-ordinated and a master swordsman…just don't start carving 'Z' on your bedroom wall!

112

Anyone for Tennis?
http://www.tennisw.com

If your dream is to hear 'Game, Set and Match' at Wimbledon, then grab your racket and get on the Net! Meet and chat with other tennis fans and learn 'smart tennis' secrets.

Armless Volleyball
http://www.sepaktakraw.com/ istaf/index.htm

'Sepaktakraw' is a team game like volleyball except you have to get the ball over the net using any part of your body except your hands or arms. Great fun!

Surf's Up Dude

http://www.sfgate.com/ sports/jenkins/surf

Stop surfing the Net and do if for real! Stay ahead of the spray with some awesome footage of surfers riding mega waves.

Black Belt

http://www.blackbeltmag.com/bbkids

If you have a question about martial arts, you can get all the answers here when you 'Ask the Masters', and you can also find classes in your area and play games and puzzles.

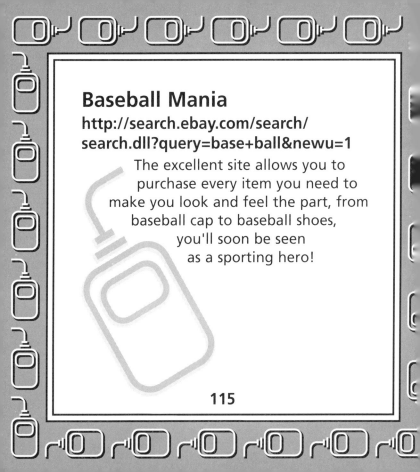

Baseball Mania
**http://search.ebay.com/search/
search.dll?query=base+ball&newu=1**

The excellent site allows you to
purchase every item you need to
make you look and feel the part, from
baseball cap to baseball shoes,
you'll soon be seen
as a sporting hero!

Jolly Hockey Sticks
http://members.aol.com/ msdaizy/sports/hockey.html

Want to know how to skate like a champ
and stay on your feet all at the same time?
You can learn how to play the game or
check out your ice hockey know-how on
this skating information site.

Cool Hockey Kids
http://www.nhl.com/kids/

Punish the puck in a speedy shockwave
game. Test your knowledge of hockey
with free printout puzzles and word
searches.

Interactive Eddie –
On the Ice He's Steady
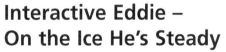
http://www.belfour.com/
interactive/interactive.htm

Are you ready for Eddie? Then skate to
the site of ice-hockey superstar Eddie, to
check out awesome stills and video clips of
his super career.

Ski World
http://www.xcskiworld.com

Full of junior cross-country skiers, there's
heart-pumping stories from the kids and a
snow-load of inspiring messages to help
get you to the winter Olympics!

Take Flight
http://www.hanglide.com

Is it a bird? Is it a plane? Is it a man with his underwear on the outside? No – it's a hand-glider! Feast your eyes on incredible pics of the experts in action and discover how it feels to jump off a mountain!

Galaxy-H
http://www.galaxy-h.gov.uk

This cool spaceship site is dedicated to keeping you healthy and safe. Visit the 'Learning Zone' for healthy food advice or the 'Recreation Zone' to find out if you are doing enough exercise!

Sportathon
http://www.sikids.com

A trainer-full of sports information written by and for kids. And if your coach is being tough on you, then get some online advice from the 'Help Column'.

Rollerblade Racing
www.rollerblade.com

Everything you need to know and more about the world of roller blading. Perfect for the novice or the professional, there is something for everyone on this site.

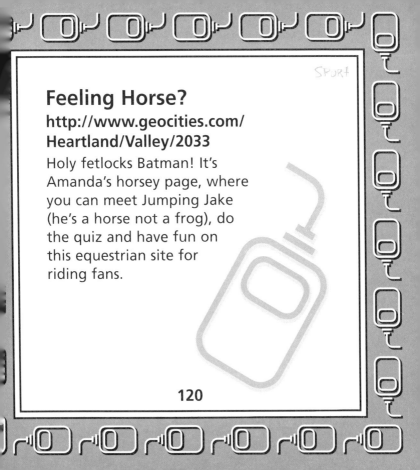

Feeling Horse?
http://www.geocities.com/Heartland/Valley/2033

Holy fetlocks Batman! It's Amanda's horsey page, where you can meet Jumping Jake (he's a horse not a frog), do the quiz and have fun on this equestrian site for riding fans.

Rope Rhymes
**http://corpcomm.net/
~gnieboer/jumprope.htm**

Know all the words to the best Jump Rope
Rhymes? If not, learn the words to over 20
here, including 'All In Together Girls' and
'Down in the Valley'.

Rack 'Em Up!
http://www.bowl.com

A one-stop bowling site that is filled with
all the latest news, info, and sporting
calendars. Although the shoes make you
look silly, this is one seriously cool site.

Cool Runnings
http://www.waycoolrunning.com

Were you born to run? Then dash to this great site for fast movers. Play the number stick game, pick up running tips and read some fast-paced running stories from other kids.

Snow Cam
http://www.rsn.com/cams

View the slopes live at this fun ski resort cam site, and check out the snowboarders and skiers doing their stuff live.

Learn the Lingo
http://www.usskiteam.com/ snowboard/sbterms.htm

Are you goofy or regular? Do you know an Alley Oop from a McEgg? If not, log on to this snowboarding language site and get with the lingo as soon as you can to stay cool on the slopes.

Backyard Olympics
http://family.go.com/ parties/events/feature/famf88games

You and your family are sure to love these backyard games that are just perfect for those long summer evenings!

Pot Black

http://www.snookernet.com

Featuring links to hundreds of other snooker sites, read the tournament reports and headline news before you pot the black!

Horses for Courses

http://www.equestriansonline.com

Mad about horses and ponies? Visit here to chat with other equestrians and see the featured stallion of the month (no, not Leonardo!).

Bocce

http://www.italiansrus.com/resources/bocceres.htm

Learn a sport here that dates back to 5000 BC in Egypt. It's called Bocce and all the rules and history can be found at this cool site.

125

Don't Look Down!
http://www.mountainzone.com

Want to feel on top of the world?
Strap on your climbing boots and join the
real-life expedition to climb the Makalu
mountain, the fifth highest in the world!

Holy Bat Cave!
http://www.cavedive.com

Come and explore a real-life underground
cave. Pore over the full-color map and
join the team of brave explorers who
dared to explore 'the farthest reaching
underground, underwater cave ever'.

Flying Machines

http://www.earlychildhood.com/crafts/
index.cfm?FuseAction=Craft&C=17

Go fly a kite! But first you have to make
one, and here is where it tells you exactly
how to do it. You'll have it up and flying
in no time!

Way High

http://www.gorp.com

Scale the mighty mountain Kilimanjaro,
known as 'the roof of Africa'. What's life
really like at 12,000 feet? (Perhaps they
just need summit to do – Groaaaan!)

Get On Your Hike
http://outdoorphoto.com/hiking

Strap on those boots, pull on a backpack and high tail it to this brilliant hiking site. You can whet your walking appetite with some fabulous scenery and, if you're a novice, there's tons of helpful advice.

Watch out! They bite
http://www.lanakids.com/summerindex.html

Yuck! This is one kind of jello you don't want to tangle with. You'll find lots of info here on these little wobbling sea monsters here and what to do if one stings you!

Hacky Sack
http://www.footbag.org

Also known as 'footbag', this great sport is only 30 years old and is basically soccer played with a beanbag! Learn the rules, how to play, and where to buy a 'footbag' right here.

Germ Warfare!
http://www.gphealthsmart.com

Calling all dirt detectives! Visit this virtual home site and stamp out germs. You can check out each room for hidden hotspots and send those little critters running for the hills!

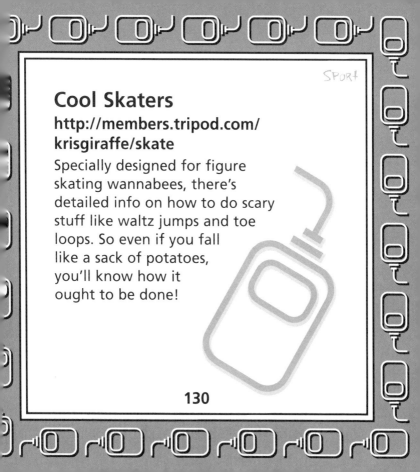

Cool Skaters
http://members.tripod.com/krisgiraffe/skate

Specially designed for figure skating wannabees, there's detailed info on how to do scary stuff like waltz jumps and toe loops. So even if you fall like a sack of potatoes, you'll know how it ought to be done!

130

Hot Shot Sport
http://www.yahooligans.com/content/sports

Juicy info and fab facts from the Yahooligans' sports board. Packed with a locker-load of information!

Wipeout!
http://tqjunior.thinkquest.org/5282/splash.shtml

How much do you really know about surfing? Take the quiz to find out and try virtual surfing! You can even learn the history of the sport as well.

Dewey Does
http://www.deweydoes.com
Dewey Does is eight years old, mad about sport, and this is his site! Join him for sporty games, toons, art, and other cool stuff.

Kidzworld
http://www.kidzworld.com
It's a kid's world, and here is a colorful and funky sports site just for kids, featuring articles on a huge mixture of your favorite sports. Read all the news and views here.

A Kick in the Grass!

http://www.playfootball.com

What's it really like to play in the National Football League? This cool new site shows you how to be a lean, mean, tackling machine – play fun games and find out the best way to run, dodge and score that touchdown!

Extreme
http://library.thinkquest.org/13857

Into extreme sports? Then visit here for the very latest trends in the word of climbing, skateboarding and inline skating at this fun and funky site.

I-Glow
http://www.i-glow.com

Girls don't sweat – they glow! So log on to this girl-friendly sports site to read your sports horoscopes and receive sports advice from resident agony aunt, Alicia.

Strange Sport
http://library.thinkquest.org/J002862

What are the weirdest sports at the Olympics beside water ballet? Log on here to find out about those sports that are so strange, they don't usually get much coverage.

Jurassic Shark
**http://www.geocities.com/
RainForest/Canopy/3018**

Fancy swimming with a Great
White Shark or hanging out
with a Hammerhead? No? You might
think differently after visiting this
impressive site! There's
full-color shark footage
(yikes!), shark cartoons,
and answers to burning
questions such as
'Do sharks have
tongues?'.

135

Dive Right In
http://members.tripod.lycos.nl/
schoonspringen/informatie/
diving_for_kids.html

This dive site is dedicated to showing you
the basics of diving and some dry-land
exercises to get you up and ready for the
next Olympic Games.

CyberCycle
http://library.thinkquest.org/10333

Visit Cogshead's Bike Shop online at this,
the ultimate biking site. It'll let you know
all the best places to ride and you can
read the history of the sport as well.

Nascar
http://www.nascar.com

The home of Nascar racing, this site includes info on the drivers, the latest news, plus games to get you in top gear in a hurry.

Anyone for Real Tennis?
http://www.real-tennis.com

Before Pete Sampras and Martina Hingis, there was the 'King of Games, Game of Kings'! Check out this exciting site on the oldest of all racket games that is still going strong!

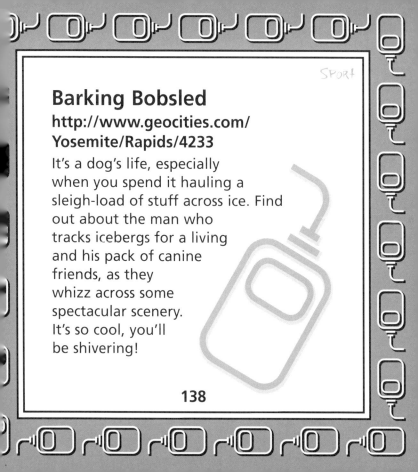

Barking Bobsled

**http://www.geocities.com/
Yosemite/Rapids/4233**

It's a dog's life, especially
when you spend it hauling a
sleigh-load of stuff across ice. Find
out about the man who
tracks icebergs for a living
and his pack of canine
friends, as they
whizz across some
spectacular scenery.
It's so cool, you'll
be shivering!

138

CyberSport
http://library.thinkquest.org/J003191

Enter the Virtual Sports Museum and find out how science plays a part in sports, how music is integrated into sports, and a whole heap of sporting history.

Kids Castle
http://www.kidscastle.si.edu

Enter the Kids Castle and meet Robinson – he plays almost every sport there is. Read sports articles and facts, look at photos, and visit the message board to have your say.

Get Gas

http://www.gas.nick.com

GAS stands for Games and Sports, and here you will find everything to do with them. Play Sports games online and learn the ins and outs of all your favorites.

Polo Land

http://polonews.com

Not just a mint with a hole in the middle, Prince Charles's favorite sport is full of drama and excitement. Log on to find all the news and views about this fast-paced game!

Three Cheers
http://www.cheeronline.com

If you've always wanted to wave a pom-pom and twirl a baton, then this site is the ultimate in cheerleader cool. Learn tips and techniques on cheerleading fitness. There's competition info, a competition corner and a message board to pass on advice to other cheerleading wannabees.

4

Games to Play

Amaze-ing
http://puzzlemaker.school.discovery.com

Cool, customized puzzle-making site for you to print out and keep. Type in your words and the computer will hide them for you in a grid of letters. Think you can find them again?

Motor Rally Alley
http://www.chevroncars.com/play/index.html

Online bumper cars for a crashing good time. Play the 'Steer Clear' race with your friends – avoid all the logs and lily pads and you might just win!

My Buddy's an Alien!
http://www.bombpop.com/main.cfm

There are tons of cool games for you to play here, including arcade games and puzzles, and there is also a section of fun crafts and coloring as well!

Arcade Village
http://www.arcadevillage.com/indexa.htm

Travel round the village and choose the games you want to play, including 'Obi', 'Space Invaders' and 'Alien Mutant Invasion'. There's also some 'two-player' games for you to play with a friend.

Yahooligans

**http://www.yahooligans.com/
content/games/index.html**

From card games to word games, there is
so much fun on this site. Find out if you
are a Chess Master or if backgammon is
more your game!

Open Sesame

**http://www.sesameworkshop.org/
oops/0,1451,rosita,00.html**

There is loads to do on this cool site.
There's a game zone, a music zone and
even a story zone. So join in the fun with
Big Bird, Elmo and friends!

High-Tech Jinks
http://www.scholastic.com/
kids/games.htm

At this high-tech site, you can play the
Cyber Speak Quiz and meet Captain
Underpants! The Harry Potter Challenge
quiz is also waiting for you – can you score
top points?

Scooby Doo's
Haunted Game Room
http://www.scoobydoobydoo.com

What's that strange noise? Is it a ghost? Or
just Shaggy's tummy rumbling? Have lots of
Hallowe'en fun with Scooby and Shaggy!

The Artist Formerly Known as Barney!
http://barneyonline.com

No, not Prince – we're talking about the famously cool purple dinosaur! Come on down to his house of fun and enjoy a game of hide-and-seek, or simply sing along.

Grammar Gorillas
http://www.funbrain.com

Make friends with the grammar gorillas and put the correct word in the right sentence, and go 'MathCar Racing' and play 'Spellaroo'. You'll have fun AND be top of your class!

Animated Bagels
http://www.acekids.com/bagels1.htm

Very sensible site – Not! Meet the
residents of Bagel City. They've
got attitude, baseball caps and a
hole in the middle! Create your very
own bagel dude, email the site
and become part of the
'Bagel Gang'. Why not
create your very own
web page of rival
muffins or a
donut family?

Game Brain
http://www.gamebrain.com
Here you will find tons of games to play,
as well as a whole host of jigsaws, puzzles,
music and stories for you to enjoy.

Be a Games Meister!
http://www.humongous.com/
Speedy kids can race with friends in a car
rally, or you could challenge Pyjama Sam to
a game of 'Checkers'. But beware! He may
wear nerdy gear but he is a champion!

'Scrabble' Supremo?
http://www.cozmos.com/jays/

For all wordy whizz kids, this is 'Scrabble' heaven. Play online with Speedy Bob and check out the sizzling 'Scrabble' links and tips.

4 Kids 2 Play
http://www.4kids2play.nl/eng

Play traditional games such as 'Memory', 'Tic Tac Toe', and 'Tangram' here, as well as some new and unusual ones, such as 'Hanoi Tower' and 'Watch Out'.

Name That Game!

http://www.demauro.com/games.html

25 games to keep you entertained for hours – ranging from trivia, to maze games to word games. Want to swap from 'Hangman' to coloring books, to a game of basketball? Then you've come to the right place!

Learning Planet

http://www.learningplanet.com/ stu/kids0.asp

Excellent fun learning games for kids. Choose a level and find a game.

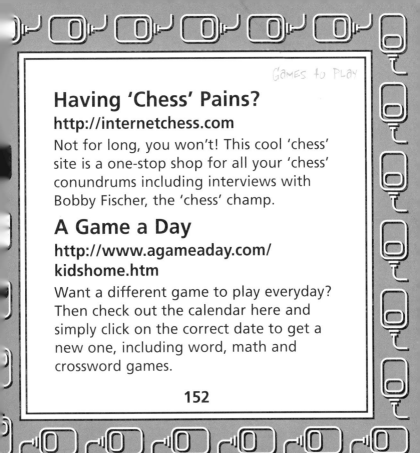

Having 'Chess' Pains?
http://internetchess.com

Not for long, you won't! This cool 'chess' site is a one-stop shop for all your 'chess' conundrums including interviews with Bobby Fischer, the 'chess' champ.

A Game a Day
http://www.agameaday.com/kidshome.htm

Want a different game to play everyday? Then check out the calendar here and simply click on the correct date to get a new one, including word, math and crossword games.

152

Ssh! – Secret Agents
http://www.thunk.com

If you want to become a secret agent, you'll need this special secret message site. Type in your message and be amazed as it's magically turned into complete gobbledygook! And for the 'Junior James Bond', you can get the scoop on how secret codes are really used.

Go Doughy-Eyed!
http://www.doughboy.com

Don't just stick your doughboy in the oven! You can play cool games with him too like 'Catch the Chocolate Chip Cookie' before he does!

Ice Cream Capers
http://www.benjerry.com/fun/

Vermont's finest have a section of games and fun stuff for you to try. Try the 'Scooper Challenge' and 'Virtual Checkers', and check out the 'Flavor Graveyard' as well.

154

Jelly Bean Kingdom
**http://www.geocities.com/
EnchantedForest/3737/**

It's a jelly bean jungle out there! Play games like 'Froggy Circus', build your own castle, or create magical faces out of thousands of your favorite jelly beans.

Oreo Fun Factory
http://www.oreo.com

Did you know that nine billion Oreo cookies are eaten every year? Hunt for the golden Oreo here and you could win a computer!

Candy Land
http://www.candystand.com/home.htm
Play your way through the candy store
arcade to win some really sweet prizes,
like 'Nintendo' or an 'Imac' computer!

Bird Splatter
and Alien Brunch!
http://www.adveract.com/
games/games.htm
Be a winged menace as you win points by
splattering people's cars. Or have fun with
the aliens who want to invade New York
in time for brunch!

156

Breakfast Bonanza Game
http://www.recorvits.com/
games/index.html

Who said you shouldn't play with your food? Help out the fat cat by slinging bacon and eggs everywhere – you win the game by making a cool face on the plate!

Goodnight Mr Snoozleberg!
http://www.cyberkids.com/fg/ga/ad/sn/

Poor old Mr Snoozleberg! He's a chronic sleepwalker and has a habit of walking out of second-floor windows wearing only his pyjamas! Can you help him through the city without letting him hurt himself?

Parallel Universe
http://www.macrayskeep.com

Looking for a role-play game with a real difference? Macray's Keep is more than just a fantasy adventure, it's a whole world where the players make up the games! So strap on your sword and go fight the forces of darkness. And if you think up a cool spell to get rid of a nasty gnome, it could end up on the web site!

Going Batty!

http://members.aol.com/
bats4kids2/boxpage1.htm

You'll go bats for this cave of flying fur balls! There are 12 fun games to choose from. Have fun finding bat homes, playing puzzles – or creating your very own batty poems on the message board.

The Beastie Game

http://www.weburbia.com/beast

Think up an imaginary beastie. It can be furry, scaly or extinct! And don't tell the computer because it has to guess what your secret beastie is.

Backgammon Galore!
http://www.bkgm.com

Backgammon is a game of luck and skill!
Log on here for the rules, places you can
play online, and even a glossary of
backgammon terms.

William Willya's Wacky Page
http://www.willya.com/
ww/choose_g.htm

Play the matching pictures game and fill in
the rhymes with William Willya and Molly.
If you like the games, you'll love the books!

Wonderland
**http://www.sonywonder.com/
wonderland**

Create sound effects! Check out the funny
sound-maker on this great site. You click
on different pictures to make a whole load
of silly sounds.

Zeeks Not Geeks
**http://zeeks.com/
Games/ZeekGames.asp**

Join the zeeky club and play board games,
word searches and brain-busting puzzles.
A whole ezine of smart stuff for smart kids.

Vagabond's Quest

http://www.netdragons.com/

Are you an Orc or a Dork? You can be anything in this brilliant fantasy game, as all your skill and cunning will be needed to complete the Vagabond's Quest.

F9 Kids

http://kids.f9.net.uk/html/games.html

Plenty of games can be found here to keep you busy, including 'Save the Spacestation' and 'Splat a Spacemole'. You can also make an alien and build 'F9 Fred'.

Buzz & Honey
http://www2.cruzio.com/~sab/buzz.html

You are Buzz and you must collect pollen
from flowers and deliver it to
Honey. However, she is fussy
where the pollen comes from, so
beware the 'Wrath of Honey'
when you play here.

Multi-Quest Bonanza
http://www.illusia.com

This is a multi-player game, so get all your friends round! Your adventure mission is 'The Quest of the Eternals'.

Pac-Man
http://www.csd.uu.se/ ~alexb/entertainment/index.html

You can't beat the old favorites, and if you visit Alexander Jean-Claude Bottema's Home Page, you can play this great classic game.

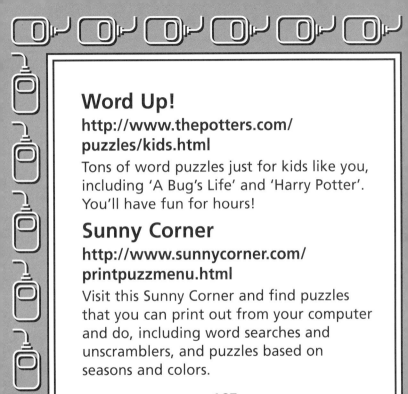

Word Up!
http://www.thepotters.com/ puzzles/kids.html

Tons of word puzzles just for kids like you, including 'A Bug's Life' and 'Harry Potter'. You'll have fun for hours!

Sunny Corner
http://www.sunnycorner.com/ printpuzzmenu.html

Visit this Sunny Corner and find puzzles that you can print out from your computer and do, including word searches and unscramblers, and puzzles based on seasons and colors.

Money, Money, Money

http://www.usmint.gov/kids/index.cfm ?FileContents=/kids/games/index.cfm

At this site owned by the US Mint, you can visit the PuzzleMint and play great games based around cash. Can you solve the 'Golden Dollar' puzzle?

Sign Language

http://www.lessontutor.com/ jmASLcross1.html

How good are you at signing? Test your knowledge with this fun sign language quiz and learn some extra words and phrases.

Do the Hokey Pokéy

http://www.geocities.com/
Area51/Crater/4784/Pokeguide.html

This amazing site is like having someone hold your hand while you walk through the different levels. If your life has gone to pieces because you can't catch a wild Pokémon, then you'll soon feel better.

Pokémon Downloads

http://www.pokemon.com/
downloads/index.html

Come and get your free Pokémon goodies! Wallpaper, badges and a screensaver are just some of the things that are up for grabs.

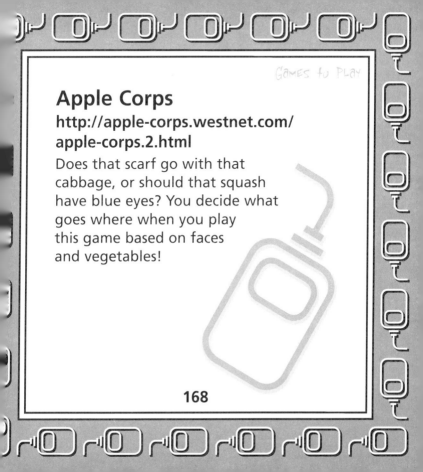

Apple Corps
http://apple-corps.westnet.com/
apple-corps.2.html
Does that scarf go with that
cabbage, or should that squash
have blue eyes? You decide what
goes where when you play
this game based on faces
and vegetables!

Billy Beaver

http://blackdog.net/billy.html

At Billy Beaver's Game Show, you can play arcade games, math and science games, card games, and board and trivia games. There's even some Pokémon!

Ben's Games

http://www.charlottebear.co.uk/games.htm

Ben, the fun games expert, has lined up some great games for you to play online, including some 3D arcade games and action and adventure games. Log on and live it up!

Punch Buggy

http://www.interlog.com/ ~csavage/punchbuggy/index.htm

Wanna ride in the Punch Buggy? Melody and Jocelyn have created this game just for you and will explain the rules to this fun road-trip game. You won't be bored on car journeys ever again.

Speedy Snails

http://home.europa.com/ ~doomer/shuskey/example1.html

Roll the dice and play the snail race. Great fun for up to six players.

Disneyland Paris
http://disneylandparis.com/uk/
introduction.htm?anim=oui

Parents are not allowed in part of this cool
site! There you will find games and
puzzles and even a section where you can
become an artist. So pick up your
paintbrush and join in the fun!

Planet Kids
http://www.planetkids.co.uk/

There is lots of cool stuff on this site. There
is a Game Showcase that has loads of games
that have different levels of difficulty. Start
off easy and see how far you get!

Fun at the Farm

**http://horsehoopranch.com/
farmfun/gamelinks.htm**

At Horsehoop Ranch, there are tons of
links to games that you can play. Simply
click on an animal and play a different
game each time.

Demoland

http://www.demoland.com

If you're not sure whether to buy a game
or not – this great site has over 400 free
downloads of the latest and greatest.
Read reviews from other kids or just play
before you buy!

Fox in Shockwave Socks!
**http://www.randomhouse.com/
seussville/games**

Seussville fans of all ages will love
these cat and fox-filled pages. Play
fresh and funny games with all your
favorite Seuss characters, or
check out what the 'Cat in
the Hat' is up to and join
in the green eggs and
ham fun!

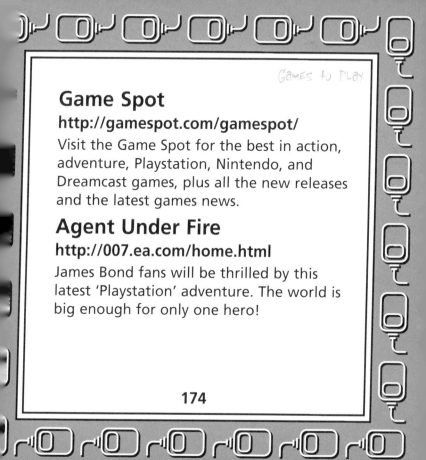

Game Spot

http://gamespot.com/gamespot/

Visit the Game Spot for the best in action, adventure, Playstation, Nintendo, and Dreamcast games, plus all the new releases and the latest games news.

Agent Under Fire

http://007.ea.com/home.html

James Bond fans will be thrilled by this latest 'Playstation' adventure. The world is big enough for only one hero!

Cool Games
http://www.etch-a-sketch.com/html/coolgames.htm

Meet Etchy and play his cool games, including an online Etch-a-Sketch, finding hidden shapes in fun pictures, plus hidden numbers and letters that need to be discovered.

Frog-tastic!
http://frogz.net/games.html

This site has gone frog-tastic! Gobble up as many flies as you can to win at 'Lickety-Splat' and download froggy wallpaper and demos.

175

Zanyfun.com
http://www.zanyfun.com.au

Here are a whole range of zany games for you to enjoy, including brainteasers, arcade games, jigsaws, and monster making games. Have fun!

Hitting a Brick Wall
http://members.aol.com/ steadle/javaduke.htm

This game is very complicated and you have to think a lot – Not! Bash the Brickie with a paddle and he knocks out the bricks. Simple huh? Well, no, not exactly! There are a few surprises in store!

Lemonade 'For Sale'
http://www.littlejason.com/lemonade/index.html

Ever wanted to own a lemonade stand? Get the lowdown on the lemonade profit war! For budding juice tycoons everywhere.

Trivia Planet
http://www.triviaplanet.com

Visit the Trivia Planet where there are tons of arcade games to play, including 'Pac Man', 'Luna Lander' and 'Defender of the Moon'. If you don't, you'll be missing out – it's out of this world.

177

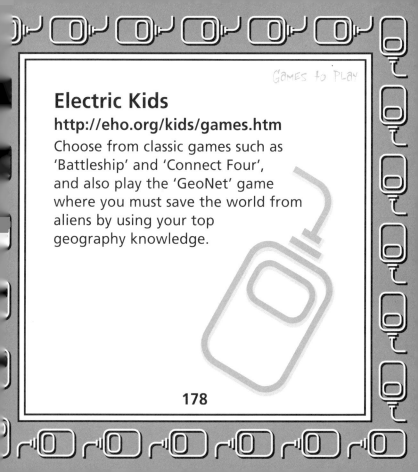

Electric Kids
http://eho.org/kids/games.htm

Choose from classic games such as
'Battleship' and 'Connect Four',
and also play the 'GeoNet' game
where you must save the world from
aliens by using your top
geography knowledge.

178

Asteroid Blaster
**http://members.aol.com/
Zstoner/Stoneroids/index.html**

Explore space and zap those asteroids with lasers. Check out the really cool explosion effects when you score a direct hit!

R U Our Kid?
http://www.ourkids.org.uk/play.asp

Play online games such as 'Falling Stars' and 'Asteroids', and Millie, the little alien, will enter your scores into the 'Hall of Fame' scoreboard. Beat others from around the world to be top of the chart!

MysteryNet
http://kids.mysterynet.com

Visit MysteryNet to discover mysteries that need solving, scary stories to read, and magic tricks to learn! Solve the 'Case of the Snack Shack' and learn how to make a card vanish into thin air.

Kids on Wheels
http://www.kidsonwheels.net/gamezone.shtml

Enter the 'Game Zone' and play 'Graffiti Art' where you can actually spray a virtual wall and create graffiti art. Get creative!

Bunny-Popping
http://www.angelfire.com/oh3/rugosab

Have fun with rabbits and puppies that love to party. These bunny-popping funsters were designed by 13-year-old Monica. Way to go, bunny girl!

The Kidz Page
http://www.thekizpage.com/freekidsgames.htm

How good is your memory? That good, huh? Well, there are memory games here to test your gray matter, as well as sports games, such as soccer, bowling and canoeing, as well as brain games, Einstein.

Joe the Dragon
**http://www.joethedragon.co.uk/
games.html**

Welcome to Joe the Dragon's lair, where
you can play games and puzzles and find
out more about Joe. You can even do
some virtual traveling!

Felix's Gameroom
**http://www.abbeville.com/
felix/games/index.htm**

In Felix's gameroom, you can pick from a
huge range of games and decide how easy
or hard you want them to be. There are
lots of games you can download!

Warning – This Site Is Fowl!
**http://www.brianmichaelsdj.com/
chicken.htm**

If cool ain't your thing – then
you can wing it with the Chicken
Dance. Say goodbye to street cred
as you follow the steps of the
silliest dance ever. This is
a move to try out with
your friends…but don't
try it on a first date!

183

No Mess, No Fuss!

http://www.mv.com/
ipusers/paintball/game

Get cyber-splattered with paint at this
amazing site – you can go watch the
games or register to play yourself.

Indy Frenzy

http://www.sikids.com/
games/indyfrenzy/index.html

There's a fine line between zoom and
doom! So steer your way carefully around a
road-hogging rookie in a monster truck and
avoid obstacles such as TVs and bathtubs,
when you play this fab racing game.

184

Trivia Blitz
http://www.puzzledepot.com/

Test your trivia knowledge on this speedy
site. The faster you answer, the more
points you win and the closer you come to
winning a prize!

Planet 'Crayola'
http://www.crayola.com/kids/

Guess how many crayons it would take to
reach the moon? Find the answer on
fun facts and play 'Crayola' games and
quizzes. Also a great story site for when
you're all colored out!

Alfie's North Pole Adventure
http://www.rooneydesign.com/AlfieAdventure.html

Follow the interactive story here and play a great game. Alfie has found a snow cave and has to go explore it to find Santa's secret workshop.

Less Gravity = More Fun
http://www.sikids.com/games/lunarshred/index.html

Our old friend Jupiter Unagi becomes a serious moon-unit zapper in this game, saving sukis and bouncing off bubble-headed sumos!

186

Anyone for Chess?

http://games.yahoo.com

Sometimes the oldies are the best! Check out this huge list of free games for you to enjoy, from 'Blackjack' to 'Bingo'.

Jumping Jupiter
http://www.sikids.com/games/snowboard/index.html

Snowboard maestro, Jupiter Unagi, will blast down anything if it has snow on it! But Japan's legendary Mount Fuji will be her biggest challenge yet. Can you help her reach the bottom safely?

5

Things to do on a Rainy Day

New to the Net?

http://webnovice.com

If you're new to the Internet, follow this friendly guide that will soon have you surfing like a pro.

The Yuckiest Site on the Net

http://www.yucky.com

This is a great fun science site with an emphasis on 'Yuck!'. Lots of squishy and disgusting fun! Take the gross-out quiz and join the yucky club and you'll also find answers to burning questions like 'Why do farts smell?'

Kite Fun

**http://www.finditquick.com/
topics/4/126/32/ttd311-fs.html**

Make a great kite in only 20 minutes when
you download the simple instructions from
the 'Big Wind Kite Factory' in Hawaii at
this breezy site.

Explore London

**http://www.explore-london.co.uk/
index.html**

This excellent site gives you details of all
the fun places to visit in London. From
Buckingham Palace to Big Ben, there is
something for everyone.

190

Bug Pin-Ups
http://www.insecta.com

Become an expert in bugs and creepy
crawlies with this full-color calendar.
There's one little critter for every month
and a full description of the horrid stuff
they do. Urrgh!

Invisible Invaders!
**http://www.pfizer.com/
rd/microbes/pagetop.html**

Meet the microbe mob. They're wriggly,
invisible germs and they're here in full
color. You can also meet Microbe Man, the
Superhero who guides you round.

Forensic Fun

**http://www.discoverlearning.com/
forensic/docs/index.html**

Help Newton the Beagle solve a baffling
mystery. Decide what he should do next
and find out some amazing info about
forensics on the way.

Dyoutinkesaurus?

**http://www.EnchantedLearning.com/
subjects/dinosaurs/allabout**

One of the best directories for dinosaur
fans. Loads of games, puzzles and bones
to sink your teeth into.

192

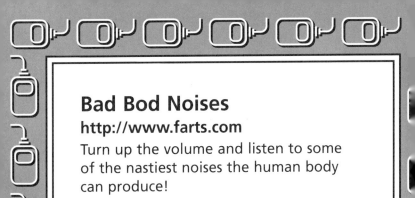

Bad Bod Noises
http://www.farts.com

Turn up the volume and listen to some of the nastiest noises the human body can produce!

Brussel Sprouts and Cabbage!
http://www.bonus.com/ bonus/search.cache/yuck.html

Check out the yuckiest food ever and share your dinnertime horrors online! What about some Japanese pizza with seaweed, squid and mayonnaise? Feeling hungry yet?

193

Cool Chef Corner
http://www.scoreone.com/kids_kitchen/

Make yourself magnificent munchies! Kids from around the world have sent in their favorite recipes for you to try.

Wild World of Wonka
http://www.wonka.com

Visit Willy Wonka's famous chocolate factory and see the surprises that await you. You can play games, color in, test your trivia knowledge, and download wallpaper...but is it lickable?

Food Secrets
http://www.topsecretrecipes.com

Did you know that the recipe to KFC's secret coating is held in an underground vault? Cool secrets of commercial recipes are revealed here every week!

Fast Fun Snacks
http://www.geocities.com/ Heartland/7997/funsnacks.htm

You'll find these wacky snacks a breeze. There are loads to choose from, like peanut butter chocolate apples and octopus sandwiches!

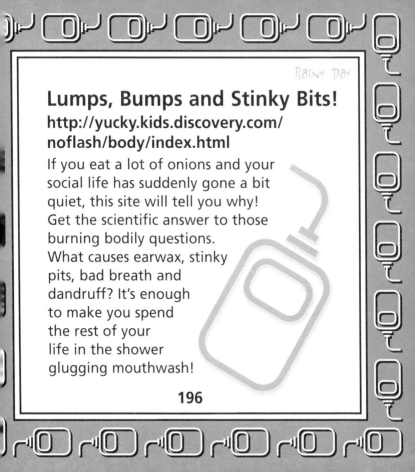

Lumps, Bumps and Stinky Bits!
http://yucky.kids.discovery.com/noflash/body/index.html

If you eat a lot of onions and your social life has suddenly gone a bit quiet, this site will tell you why! Get the scientific answer to those burning bodily questions. What causes earwax, stinky pits, bad breath and dandruff? It's enough to make you spend the rest of your life in the shower glugging mouthwash!

Build Your Own Volcano!

**http://hometown.aol.com/
ckckside/reports/volcanoes/vol1.htm**

Build an exploding volcano with stuff you can find lying around the house. Yes, really! For lava lovers, there's lots of links to groovy sites about real volcanoes.

Be a Magician

http://www.conjuror.com/magictricks/

If you're just starting off in the world of magic, you'll love these free tricks to keep up your sleeve – literally! Try the 'self-tying handkerchief' trick or the 'coin through the elbow' trick.

Diamond Jim

http://www.diamond-jim.com/magic

Miracles can happen across the Net.
Well, card miracles anyway! Pick a card,
any card, and prepare to be amazed as
Diamond Jim reads your mind.

Indian Water Trick

**http://www.angelfire.com/
pe/SimpleMagik/**

Astound your friends with the famous
Indian water trick. User-friendly
instructions on what the audience sees,
what you need and how the trick actually
happens!

Mental Magic
**http://www.teleport.com/
~jrolsen/index.shtml**

The Great Mysto claims he can read your mind. Have great fun picking a character and he tries to guess who it is!

Color It!
http://www.kiddonet.com

Where can you create graffiti art without getting into trouble with adults? Why here, of course! There are also interactive comics, facts about animals, jokes and plenty of games for you to enjoy.

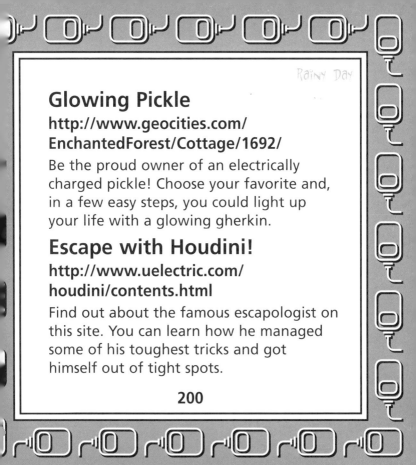

Rainy Day

Glowing Pickle
**http://www.geocities.com/
EnchantedForest/Cottage/1692/**

Be the proud owner of an electrically
charged pickle! Choose your favorite and,
in a few easy steps, you could light up
your life with a glowing gherkin.

Escape with Houdini!
**http://www.uelectric.com/
houdini/contents.html**

Find out about the famous escapologist on
this site. You can learn how he managed
some of his toughest tricks and got
himself out of tight spots.

200

The Man and His Magic
http://www.dcopperfield.com
This is the official site of the magical showman, David Copperfield. Learn some online magic and vote for the best Copperfield illusion.

Surf Monkey
http://www.surfmonkey.com
This is one cool site, where you can go on adventures with the Surf Monkey! You can listen to music, read cartoons, check out the cyberfriend communicator, and enter the 3D chatroom.

Rainy Day

Monster in Training!
**http://www.geocities.com/
Heartland/7134/Halloween/halfun.htm**

This is the page where saucy spirits and
ghosties gather to frighten the life out of
you! Check out the spooky riddles.

Your Own Haunted Castle
**http://www.nationalgeographic.com/
features/97/castles/enter.html**

Name your castle and enter through the
creaky drawbridge. Then follow Marcus
the Mouse as you explore the dark and
dusty dungeons! Who or 'What' will
you find?

Monster Begone
http://www.monsterbegone.com
This brilliant site gives you all the help you need to get rid of ghosties, ghoulies and all the other nighttime pests who are lurking under your bed!

Animal Magic
http://www.animaland.org
If you love animals, you'll love 'Animal Land' which is full of tips on how to care for your pets, has animal stories for you to read, and also teaches you about animal jobs for when you get bigger.

Rainy Day

Space Place
http://spaceplace.jpl.nasa.gov/spacepl.htm

Visit the 'Space Place' and find tons of spacey things to make as well as lots of spacey things to do.

Are You a Dragon or a Goat?
http://www.dae.com/cny/links.html#zodiac

What Chinese animal reveals your personality type? There are 12 Chinese horoscope animals and you're one of them – be grateful there's no Year of the Slug!

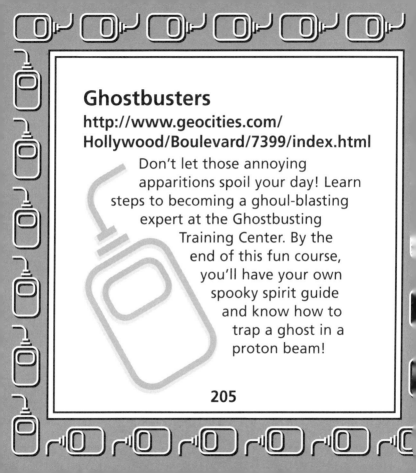

Ghostbusters

http://www.geocities.com/Hollywood/Boulevard/7399/index.html

Don't let those annoying apparitions spoil your day! Learn steps to becoming a ghoul-blasting expert at the Ghostbusting Training Center. By the end of this fun course, you'll have your own spooky spirit guide and know how to trap a ghost in a proton beam!

Rainy Day

Talk to the Animals
**http://www.cyberark.com/
animal/telepath.htm**

This site for budding Dr Doolittles is all
about how animals 'talk', and if we can talk
back? Check out the dolphin expert who
claims to have decoded their language!

Build-a-Monster
http://www.goobo.com

Create your very own monster by choosing
a head, mid-section, and legs from a wide
range. Then you can creep up and frighten
all your friends!

206

Dr Kid
http://www.kidsdoctor.com

Who said you can't get a doctor to make house calls? Have your very own doctor on hand at this award-winning site. Get the answers to medical questions you've always wanted to ask.

Create Your Own Alien
http://www.alienexplorer.com/ createalien/home.html

Let Mr Ducker, the kooky science teacher, show you how to create your very own space creature. Loads of little green links to other alien sites!

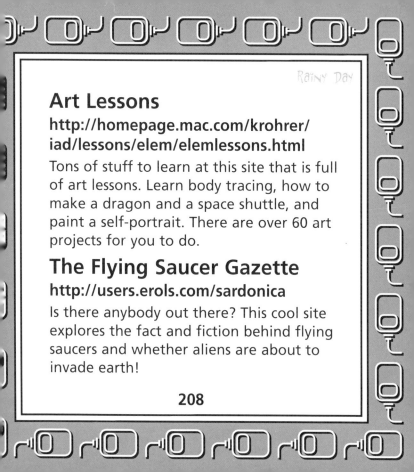

Art Lessons

**http://homepage.mac.com/krohrer/
iad/lessons/elem/elemlessons.html**

Tons of stuff to learn at this site that is full
of art lessons. Learn body tracing, how to
make a dragon and a space shuttle, and
paint a self-portrait. There are over 60 art
projects for you to do.

The Flying Saucer Gazette

http://users.erols.com/sardonica

Is there anybody out there? This cool site
explores the fact and fiction behind flying
saucers and whether aliens are about to
invade earth!

The Truth Is Out There!
http://www.sev.com.au/
toonzone/sevfiles.asp

Very funny comic strip spoof of 'The
X-Files'. Read about the exploits of agents
Mouldy and Scurvy and their mission to
track down aliens.

Strange But True
http://www.improb.com/

Be amazed by some crackpot scientific
research – like the long study on the
effects of winking, and research into feline
reactions to bearded men!

Rainy Day

Get On Board
http://www.androidpubs.com
Got $2,000,000 to spare? You too could go to Mars then on the holiday of a lifetime. Check out the groovy pics of your intergalactic destination!

Kendra's Krayons Coloring Book
http://www.geocities.com/ EnchantedForest/7155
An interactive virtual coloring book that lets you choose what picture you want to color in. Select a color from the palette and get coloring!

Big Rubber Ball

**http://www.easttexas.com/
pdlg/theball.htm**

Why would anyone want to make a huge
ball out of rubber bands? Don't ask silly
questions! Check out the story of two
nutty guys who collect rubber bands to
fulfil their dream.

Museum of Bad Art

http://www.glyphs.com/moba

Enter the bad art virtual gallery and learn
the crushing truth that just because you
feel it, doesn't mean you can paint it!

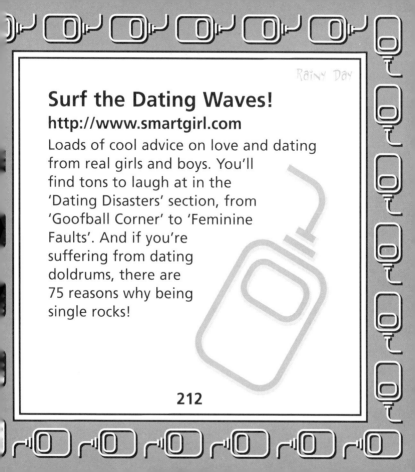

Surf the Dating Waves!
http://www.smartgirl.com

Loads of cool advice on love and dating from real girls and boys. You'll find tons to laugh at in the 'Dating Disasters' section, from 'Goofball Corner' to 'Feminine Faults'. And if you're suffering from dating doldrums, there are 75 reasons why being single rocks!

Kids Courier
http://www.kidscourier.com

This fun newspaper features games, trivia, writing, and news and reviews, all aimed at kids just like you! Make sure you visit Wilbur's World and maybe try climbing Mt Brilliant.

Kidz Draw
http://www.kidzdraw.com

In this site dedicated to art, you can create collages, learn about great artists' lives, send samples of your work to the editor, and read interviews with famous illustrators.

Rainy Day

The Clubhouse
http://cbc4kids.com
Join 'The Clubhouse' and visit this one-stop shop of jokes, songs, stories, and poems. There is also a 'Pet Arena', games, and TV program info. In fact, there is so much to do, you won't even notice that you've missed lunch!

Wired Owl
http://www.owlkids.com
If you are aged six to nine, Chick and Dee are looking forward to meeting you and give you 'optical illusions' and jokes to enjoy.

Where Are My Pants?

http://www.sock-monkey.com/pants.html

So that's why you couldn't find your jeans! Be convinced, O Sceptical One, and check out this hilarious trouser-snatching site.

Spoon Bender!

http://www.uri-geller.com

Focus your mind on the official Uri Geller homepage. Check out his photo gallery, featuring himself surrounded by thousands of bendy spoons. Bet that's the last time he'll be allowed to borrow the cutlery!

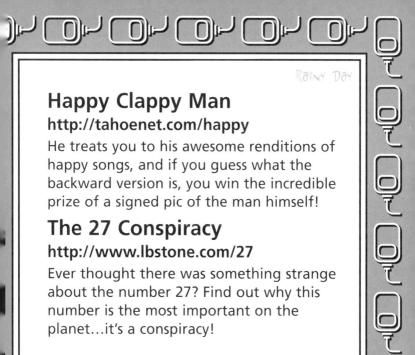

Rainy Day

Happy Clappy Man
http://tahoenet.com/happy
He treats you to his awesome renditions of happy songs, and if you guess what the backward version is, you win the incredible prize of a signed pic of the man himself!

The 27 Conspiracy
http://www.lbstone.com/27
Ever thought there was something strange about the number 27? Find out why this number is the most important on the planet…it's a conspiracy!

216

Now You See It...
http://www.illusionworks.com

Literally hours and hours of cool material here all about the art of illusion. Check out the brilliant interactive demonstrations!

Sci-Fi Cookbook
**http://www.geocities.com/
Area51/Dimension/3161/SFC/list.html**

Try your hand at 'Hobbit Hash' or 'Chicken Fried Godzilla Lips'. There are hundreds to choose from – the only problem is that some of the ingredients might be hard to come by!

Lego Club
http://www.lego.com/games

Here you will find over 25 games to keep you amused, including 'Dino Pig', where you have to build a dinosaur from its bones, and 'Shark Attack', where you have to try and keep the shark in the river.

The Poorly Drawn Lamp Page
http://www.geocities.com/ SoHo/Lofts/8112/lamppage.htm

If you can't draw, send in your artistic impressions of a lamp. They'll print anything and the badder, the better!

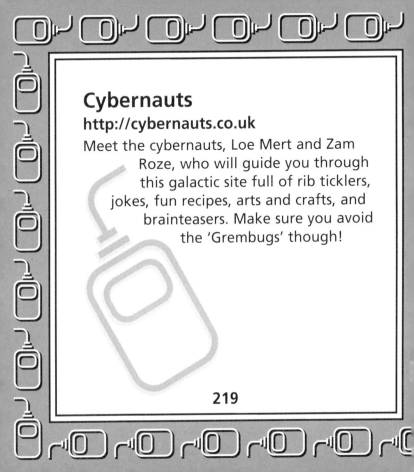

Cybernauts
http://cybernauts.co.uk

Meet the cybernauts, Loe Mert and Zam Roze, who will guide you through this galactic site full of rib ticklers, jokes, fun recipes, arts and crafts, and brainteasers. Make sure you avoid the 'Grembugs' though!

Stamp Out Furby!
**http://www.jelloboy.com/
stomp_furby/DEFAULT.HTM**

Should the furry little Furby be saved or
stamped on? Only you can decide – thumbs
up or thumbs down? You can also choose
to visit the virtual 'Taco Bell' center!

Chat on Easy Street
**http://www.legalpadjr.com/
schedule.htm**

Multi-chat room designed for kids to talk
and share interests with their own age
group. Tons of clubs and chat rooms to
enjoy.

Kids on the Web
**http://www.brookes.ac.uk/
rms/kidsontheweb/**

If you are not used to using the Internet,
this is a cool site to help you get
comfortable with the web. You can learn
the technical terms and how to surf the
site to find what you want.

Marius's Cow Tipping Page
**http://www.blueneptune.com/
~maznliz/tipcow.shtml**

If your burning ambition has been to
tip a virtual cow, don't let anything stand
in the way of your dream!

Uproar
http://www.amused.com/

Let there be fun! Uproar has a whole site full of fun for you, including 'Name That Tune', 'Wild Cards' for you to send to your family and friends, and 'Animation Station', which features great cartoons.

Formal Fork Frenzy
http://www.westernsilver.com/ etiquette.html

Impress your parents with some fine and fancy table manners. Know which fork is supposed to go where and pick up some tips on etiquette.

Kids' World
http://www.kidsworld-online.com

This is the online version of the '*KidsWorld*' magazine, and is full of contests, games, news, and links to other cool sites to keep you amused for hours when it's raining outside.

Wic-Kid
http://www.wic-kid.com

If you are a wic-kid kid, you can solve the travel-related mystery to be found at this fun-flying site. Find out about the funny face stamped on airplane windows and play games.

223

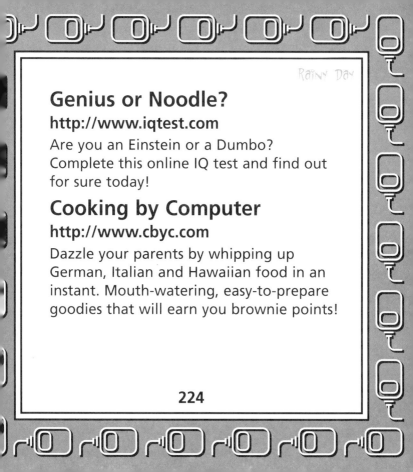

Rainy Day

Genius or Noodle?
http://www.iqtest.com

Are you an Einstein or a Dumbo? Complete this online IQ test and find out for sure today!

Cooking by Computer
http://www.cbyc.com

Dazzle your parents by whipping up German, Italian and Hawaiian food in an instant. Mouth-watering, easy-to-prepare goodies that will earn you brownie points!

Graffiti Wall
http://www.kidscom.com/ orakc/newwall/indexright.html

Scribble all over this wall of words! All you have to do is register and kids from all over the world will read your words as fast as you can write them!

The Headbone Zone
http://www.headbone.com/ features/scopes

This chat room is a bit different – meet other kids who are interested in the same things as you! In the 'Act Out' studio they even have dances and cruises.

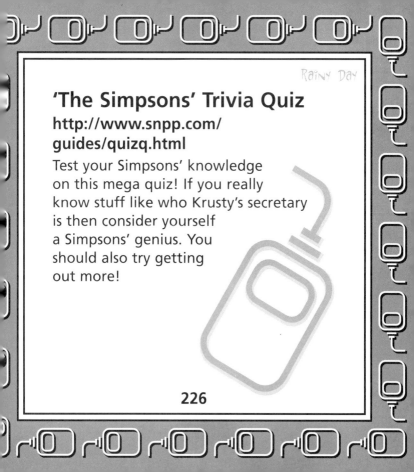

Rainy Day

'The Simpsons' Trivia Quiz
**http://www.snpp.com/
guides/quizq.html**

Test your Simpsons' knowledge
on this mega quiz! If you really
know stuff like who Krusty's secretary
is then consider yourself
a Simpsons' genius. You
should also try getting
out more!

226

Blooming Marvellous
http://www.virtualflowers.com

Send a beautiful bunch of cyber blooms for free! Choose from seven bouquets, add your message and your floral fan letter will be on its way!

Dynamo Digital Messages!
http://www.mamamedia.com/activities/webcards

Check out how you can make up your own digital greeting cards. You pick an animation, a greeting and fill in your own message – much cooler than just sending email!

227

Works of Art
http://www.geocities.com/SoHo/7373/

Why send ordinary emails when you can send groovy arty ones for free! Download some of these full color images and jazz up the text to amaze your friends.

Homer the Great!
http://www.geocities.com/ TelevisionCity/Set/3669

Not the Greek guy, the really famous one! This award-winning site has the Daddy of all Simpsons doing what he does best – eating donuts and shouting a lot! Doh!

Death-like Blasters
http://www.createafart.com

Embarrass all your friends by emailing customized bodily noises to them! Choose from Death-Like Blasters and Long Stinky Rippers!

Going Dotty!
http://www.xs4all.nl/ ~spaanszt/Domino_Plaza.html

Visit this site to find out about virtually any domino game on earth. Play them all and even discover loads of info about the domino-tipping craze.

229

Animabets
http://www.animabets.com

Dudley the Daredevil Duck, Tyrone
Tyrannosaurus, and a host of other animal
friends are waiting for you to come to
their site for lots of activities and fun.
Learn all about cooking, self-defense and
disguises.

Sneaker Freak
http://www.sneakers.pair.com

Charlie is crazy about sneakers and this is
his web site. Check out the photo gallery
and the entire history of this 'can't-live-
without' footwear. Find the latest here!

Tinkle the Ivories
http://www.pianoworld.com
This site contains everything you need to know about learning the piano, and includes music biz news and fun facts!

Pet Care
http://www.avma.org/care4pets/
We all love our pets but do we look after them properly? This web site answers all your veterinary questions and gives advice on making sure your pets stay healthy and happy!

Rainy Day

My Daily Paper
http://www.crayon.net

Imagine being a media tycoon...well, now
the dream can become a reality at this
site, which allows you to create your own
daily newspaper!

Rainbow Ridge
http://www.rainbow-ridge.org/
index2.html

The town of Rainbow Ridge has a
population of 65 but you are welcome
to visit whenever you want for online
coloring, a great soundtrack, and links to
other fun sites for cyberkids.

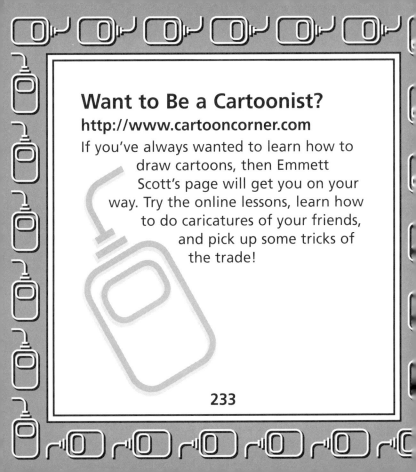

Want to Be a Cartoonist?
http://www.cartooncorner.com

If you've always wanted to learn how to draw cartoons, then Emmett Scott's page will get you on your way. Try the online lessons, learn how to do caricatures of your friends, and pick up some tricks of the trade!

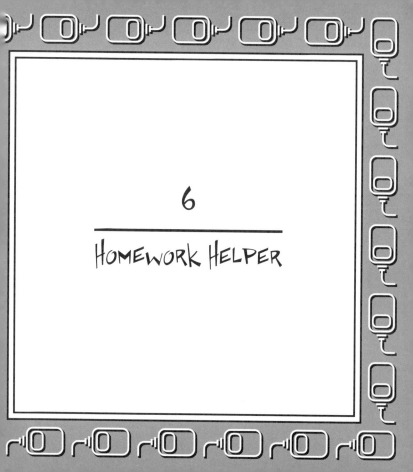

6

HOMEWORK HELPER

Wise Guy
http://www.askanexpert.com/

Are you having homework hell? Check out this friendly selection of online super tutors who will soothe your troubled brow. If they can't help, they sure know a site that can!

A, B, C...Er, What's Next?
http://www.enchantedlearning.com/ Dictionary.html

A great illustrated dictionary where words are used in sentences, so that you can see how they work!

Clever Clogs
http://www.studyweb.com
Like having a clever pal sitting next to you who knows all the answers. From Anatomy to Zoology, this vast reference site will help you finish your homework faster. Hurrah!

Discovery School
http://school.discovery.com/ homeworkhelp/bjpinchbeck/index.html
There are plenty of homework helpers at this site, but it also has other fun things to do such as creating puzzles, searching the 'Clip Art Gallery' and having a go at the 'Brain Boosters'.

KidsClick

http://sunsite.berkeley.edu/KidsClick!

Over 600 links to all kinds of fascinating subjects can be found here, so that you can find out about everything from board games to machinery.

Mama Media

http://www.mamamedia.com

At this one-stop info shop, you will learn loads of facts and can link to virtual museum tours, including the Louvre in Paris, which you can visit from the comfort of your own home!

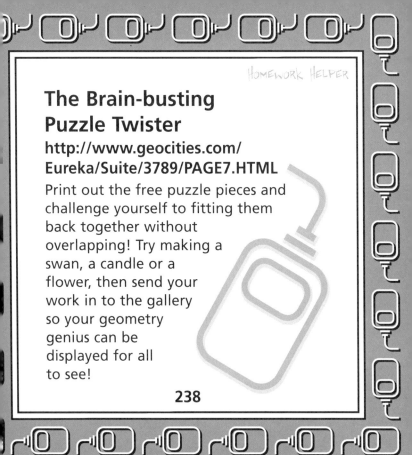

The Brain-busting Puzzle Twister

http://www.geocities.com/ Eureka/Suite/3789/PAGE7.HTML

Print out the free puzzle pieces and challenge yourself to fitting them back together without overlapping! Try making a swan, a candle or a flower, then send your work in to the gallery so your geometry genius can be displayed for all to see!

A+ Math

http://www.aplusmath.com

Want an A+ in math? Then visit a site developed to help you, and improve your math skills. There are online flashcards and worksheets to help you, and a homework helper to check your math solutions.

U Rule School

http://www.youruleschool.com/

This is the place where the students do exactly what they like! Get yourself a nickname, a locker and run down those cyber halls to the 'Laugheteria' and the 'Yumnasiam'. There's no homework either!

Spice It Up
http://www.uselessknowledge.com

If you're looking for an inspired quote or a random factoid to zip up that assignment, then this site has over 10,000 nuggets of gold dust to give your assignment that little something extra.

The Power of Words
http://www.thesaurus.com

This is a quick and easy *Roget's Thesaurus* – if you have a question about spelling, grammar, or language, it gives you examples and related words. Couldn't be easier!

Flashcard Fantastic
http://www.aplusmath.com

Test your knowledge of mathematics with these colorful funky flashcards. You can check out your progress on addition, subtraction and multiplication with the aid of games such as 'Bingo'!

Monster Math
http://lifelong.com

Practice your counting skills and find out what lurks in Dred's closet. The monsters need your help in counting their body parts! These amazing story pages are packed with fun math challenges.

241

Wall Street Whizz Kids
http://www.younginvestor.com

Learn how to be a cool cash dude and have fun investing money. Yes, really! Start with the basics and find out how to make your allowance grrrowww!

Money Made Easy
http://www.kidsbank.com/ index_3.html

You're never too young (or old) to learn about money or how banks work, so find out with this bank designed exclusively for kids! All that complicated money stuff is described in an easy-to-understand way.

The Saving Lab
http://www.plan.ml.com/family/kids

Wouldn't it be great to be able to buy that new game or toy without having to crawl to your parents? Well check out how you can with 'Savin' Dave'.

Kids' Place
http://www.eduplace.com/kids

Join Gus, Roz, Dobie and Ruby for fun activities and games to help you get to grips with math, reading, social studies and science. Learning shouldn't be this much fun!

Algebra Online
http://www.algebra-online.com

If you're suffering from algebra angst, then check out the free tutor to help you along! There's loads of advice and examples to clear your brain, or you could post your problems on the message board.

Mrs Glossar's Math Goodies
http://www.mathgoodies.com/lessons

Mrs Glosser is a really nice math teacher, so check out her shapes and percentages. She doesn't give you a hard time if you get it wrong, so get some number know-how!

244

Zoom School

http://www.enchantedlearning.com/school/index.shtml

Grab your books and have fun learning at this colorful school where you're never made to stay behind. It's geared towards a monthly theme like geography or history, so you can get the lowdown on new subjects all the time.

245

Feels Like Fun
http://www.period.com/puzzles

Here's the challenge! Can you connect four dots with eight straight lines? Or how many fruity 'Skittles' can you get into your mouth at once? This funky game site will have you thinking like a mathematician without even realizing it!

Keep Watching the Skies
http://www.skypub.com/tips/tips.shtml

Everything the junior astronomer needs! If you want to know how to use or buy a telescope, you can find all the answers here.

Stephen Hawking – Trekkie!
http://www.psyclops.com/hawking

Yes, it's true! Learn about time, space and black holes with Stephen Hawking, the brilliant physicist. Ask the genius himself about the universe and everything!

They're Alive, Doctor!
http://www.cellsalive.com

Learn lots about those red-and-white things floating about inside you! This site is all about blood cells – and how they fight disease.

It's a Chemical Thing
http://www.chem4kids.com

What's that stuff you live and breathe? Apart from Pokémon? It's called oxygen – learn all about it here, along with gas, solid, liquid, and plasma, in this easy-to-follow reference guide.

Wonderful World of Science
http://www.explorescience.com

Is it true that a watched pot never boils? Now you can find out with this great time estimation section! There are loads of cool science facts, all connected to everyday stuff that you can relate to.

Rhyme Zone
http://www.rhymezone.com

Need to come up with a poem for school fast? Then visit the 'Rhyme Zone' where you type in a word to find its rhymes and definitions. Impress that teacher!

Ultimate Mad Scientist
http://www.westegg.com/einstein

Next time you think you're no good at science, remember that Albert Einstein was called a dunce at school! It's true! Find out all about him here.

Eat My Asteroids!

http://www.kidscience.about.com

Well, you always knew that asteroids were made of mashed potato, didn't you? Make some spacy potato cakes and find out why those little lumps of rock just keep on coming!

Out of This World

http://www.seds.org/ nineplanets/nineplanets

Learn more about space with this great intergalactic cybertour of our Solar System, including all the planets and their moons. Great music too!

Dr Math
http://mathforum.com/dr.math
Any math question you can possibly think
of can be answered at this site by the
amazing Dr Math. No question is too easy
or too hard!

Absolutely Animals
http://www.birminghamzoo.com/ao
If you're trying to track down a beastie,
this great site can help you find all the
info you need. It's an A–Z guide with lots
of big furry links!

Body Bits

http://www.innerbody.com

Terrific full-color interactive site that shows how bits of you work and how you're put together. Respect is due!

All the Answers

http://www.acekids.com/ homework.html

If you are desperate for help with your homework, you can email the experts at ACE Kids for all the answers. You can even sign up to help others as a homework helper yourself!

252

Muscle Magic
http://danke.com/kidsmuscles/kidmuscle1.html

Flex those muscles and find out how each one of them works. There's cool animation and advice on how to build those muscles up. Work it, baby!

Math Baseball
http://www.funbrain.com/math

Make math more fun by learning to play math baseball at this site. It will improve your math too – it couldn't be easier!

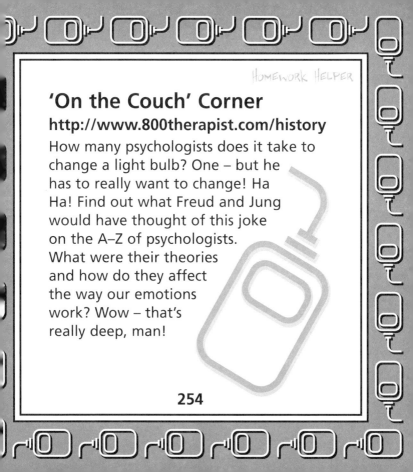

'On the Couch' Corner
http://www.800therapist.com/history

How many psychologists does it take to change a light bulb? One – but he has to really want to change! Ha Ha! Find out what Freud and Jung would have thought of this joke on the A–Z of psychologists. What were their theories and how do they affect the way our emotions work? Wow – that's really deep, man!

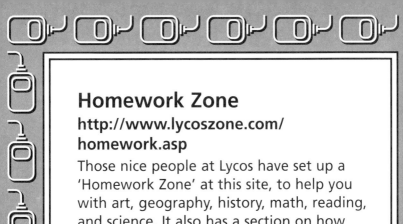

Homework Zone
http://www.lycoszone.com/ homework.asp

Those nice people at Lycos have set up a 'Homework Zone' at this site, to help you with art, geography, history, math, reading, and science. It also has a section on how stuff works and a translation facility.

'And the Nominations Are…'
http://www.almaz.com

This is a brilliant and inspirational site about the Nobel Prize. Find out who won and what for, and maybe one day it'll be your name that's read out!

Pet Doctor

http://www.thepetdoctor.com/welcome.htm

If you need some fast advice about your sick pet – it's here, it's free, and it's from a qualified vet.

Homework Spot

http://www.homeworkspot.com

Here you can get help in tons of subjects but it also has fun things too, like a field trip section – visit the 'Baseball Hall of Fame', the Amazon rainforest, and a chocolate factory!

What Do They Do?

http://www.webquarry.com/~lgfd/

Great A–Z site of different careers, from Acting to Zoology. You can find out what each job entails and there's a career story to go with each site.

What Shall I Do with My Life?

http://www.careerexperience.com

If you need some help with direction in life, this job-busting site helps you to match career ideas with what you like to do. Believe it or not, the idea is for you to earn your living doing something you enjoy and this site shows you how!

257

Learn Sign Language
**http://members.aol.com/
SignChoir/index.html**

This is a cool and unique site that has
songs, poems and stories all in sign
language…and if you don't already know
how to sign, this is the place to learn.

Fact Monster
http://www.factmonster.com/homework

Somewhere out there is the Fact Monster,
waiting for you to visit him. He will then
send you to sites that will help you
develop your listening and speaking skills,
and improve your writing technique.

258

Pre-School Fun
http://preschooleducation.com
Join your very own pre-school online.
Tons of projects, reading and writing tips,
a message board and a fun room where
you can take a break and hear some jokes!

Groovy Grammar Clinic
http://www.edunet.com/
english/grammar/index.cfm
Scroll through the table of contents to
find the subject index and zap those
grammar gremlins. Check out the helpful
grammar clinic to sort your pronouns
from your protons.

Kids' Planet
http://www.kidsplanet.org

This is your planet, so it is your duty to learn all you can about it. Here you will find fun factsheets on animals and wildlife, and there are even some games to play so that it isn't all hard work!

Writers' Den
http://www2.actden.com/writ_den

Be the classroom bard with this practical workshop on writing techniques. Check out how you can make your sentences sharper and your essays more energetic!

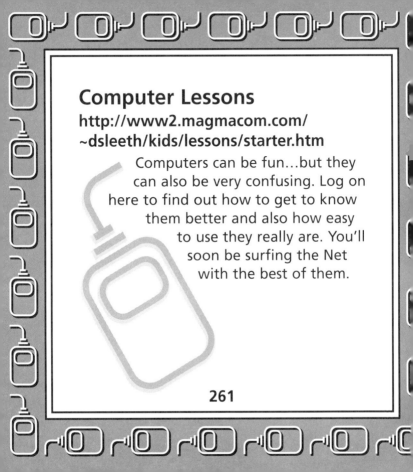

Computer Lessons
http://www2.magmacom.com/ ~dsleeth/kids/lessons/starter.htm

Computers can be fun...but they can also be very confusing. Log on here to find out how to get to know them better and also how easy to use they really are. You'll soon be surfing the Net with the best of them.

261

African-American History
http://www.kn.pacbell.com/
wired/BHM/AfroAm.html

Check out this site for the amazing history
of African-American culture. Take part in
the interactive treasure hunt and test your
knowledge on the quiz!

Cybersleuth Kids
http://cybersleuth-kids.com

Great kids' directory for hunting out
homework help sites from history to news
and media, plus fun sites and web design
links.

Classic Books Bonanza
http://www.shared-visions.com/
explore/literature

Explore an entire universe of great classic
books written over the last 500 years.

Author, Author!
http://www.blupete.com/
Literature/Biographies/Literary/
BiosFiction.htm

Bursting biographical site that contains just
about everyone who ever wrote a classic.
Check out the extracts and quotes and find
out the most important facts.

Clay-brained Footlicker!
http://www.geocities.com/Athens/ Acropolis/4226/humanities/insults.html

Yes, now you too can be rude with a cool Shakespearean insult kit! Just take a couple of words from the three columns and stick 'Thou' on the end. Easy!

Atlapedia
http://www.atlapedia.com

If you need a map in a hurry, or need to know where Hong Kong is in the quickest time poss!, then this is the site for you.

How to Read Music
**http://datadragon.com/
education/reading**

If you couldn't tell a treble clef from a
triple burger, find out the basics of
reading music on this great site. It's clear
and explains in a fun, easy-to-follow way.

Play That Didgeridoo!
http://www.rdrop.com/~mulara

It's an Australian instrument that's
surrounded by myth and legend, and here
you can find out about its amazing history
and learn to play it too!

Drama Queen?
http://www.vl-theatre.com
This site is a one-stop shop for all theater lovers. You can track down every single play in print and all the theater companies in the world.

The Twang 'n' String Site
http://www.guitarstuff.com
If you love the guitar, you'll love the free lessons on this site and the huge section on some of the great guitarists of our time.

Arty Galleries
http://www.artlex.com

Huge and totally excellent site on the oily
world of art. Visit the largest virtual art
gallery in the world – or use it as a
springboard to other art-related sites.

Stinky Poetry!
http://members.aol.com/
zamphir1/poetmain.htm

If you've had enough literary genius,
check out this truly terrible poetry site.
Swoon to the poem about the penguin,
or the meaningful 'Ode to Pants'!

Show Art

http://www.naturalchild.com/gallery

Send your masterpiece to this huge site of young people's art. Kids from all over the world have contributed to this fabulous site, so you'll be in good artistic company.

Cyberhaunts

http://www.freenet.hamilton.on.ca/ ~aa937/Profile.html

This helpful site has everything you need to know, from animals to literature. It even teaches you how to create your own web page, and has links to other cool kids, sites and music you can download.

Today in History
http://www.scopesys.com/anyday
Pick any day of the year and the computer will come up with all the amazing history that happened on that date. Who was born and what happened?

Greek Hit and Myth
http://www.messagenet.com/myths
This excellent site tries to separate the facts from the legends surrounding those guys in togas. Try the fun quiz – if you thought a Dryad was something to do with plumbing, you definitely need this site!

Triumph of the Nerds!
**http://www.digitalcentury.com/
encyclo/update/comp_hd.html**

Did you know that the first
computer was invented about
5000 years ago? Trace its history and
development, and where they are
headed in the future. And
you know those geeky
types who were always
fiddling with
computers? Check
out how rich they
are now!

270

The Tower of London
http://www.tower-of-london.com/

Enter ye olde Tower of London! You can take a virtual tour of the Crown Jewels, the dungeon or take a look at the great Scaffold Speeches – a collection of the last words of the condemned.

Got Homework?
http://eggboy.freeservers.com/ school/got.htm

If you desperately need help with that dreaded homework, the sites listed here will be able to help you. You can also take part in the homework poll, and have your say.

271

World Leaders
http://www.geocities.com/ Athens/1058/rulers.html

Great reference site for world leaders of the past 100 years – you can search by country or by year to get all the info about the world leader of your choice.

Robin Hood – Was He Good?
http://www.geocities.com/ Athens/Acropolis/4198/rh/index.html

Who was Robin Hood and why were his men merry? Check out this cool site all about the real Robin...no relation to Batman!

Mammoth Museum
http://www.mammothsite.com

Take part in one of the world's greatest fossil hunts – for a 23,000-year-old mammoth. Join the dig for this four-legged, prehistoric frozen dinner, complete with trunk and tusks!

Studying Stress Buster
http://www.1stkids.com/jokes.html

What's the difference between a train and a teacher? To find out, go to this rib-tickling site of jokes sent in by kids who are just as fed up with their homework as you are!

Hyper History
**http://www.hyperhistory.com/
online_n2/History_n2/a.html**

This fantastic history site covers over 3000 years of history, coded into clear sections such as culture, science and religion. So if it isn't here, then it probably didn't happen!

Go the Distance!
http://www.indo.com/distance

Are you dying to find out the distance between London and Bali? All you have to do is enter two locations and the computer will quickly come back with the exact distance between the two. Cool!

274

Eggy's World
http://www.eggysworld.com/links/edulinks.htm

Eggy will point you in the direction of great learning sites when you log on here, and will also give you a good description of what you will find when you get there.

Triple A Math
http://www.aaamath.com

Learn at your own pace at this site that gives help on every math subject imaginable, including decimals, percentages and statistics.

275

World Wars
http://www.search-beat.com/worldwar.htm

This is a massive site on World War I with links to sites on World War II. It's crammed with information, footage to download, and newspaper articles from *The Times*.

Algebra Online
http://www.algebra-online.com

Make life easy for yourself! This isn't a fun subject but help is at hand at this site specifically designed to hone your algebra skills.

Languages for Travelers
http://www.travlang.com/languages

Picture the scene. You're in France and you don't know how to ask for a donut. The nightmare is over because this cool site gives you enough vocabulary in any language to survive in over 70 countries! Select the language you want and find out the important words and phrases you need, such as 'Ou sont les toilettes?'!

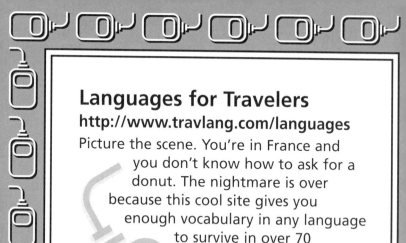

277

Train Your Parents!
http://www.e-score.com

Horrible homework? Well, why should you suffer alone? This tells you how to get your parents involved. Steer them to this site, which will give them advice on how to take a more 'active' role in your education!

Q&As
http://www.allexperts.com

Ask any question you need the answer to – from computer know-how right through to religion. All you need to know or find out is right here!

278

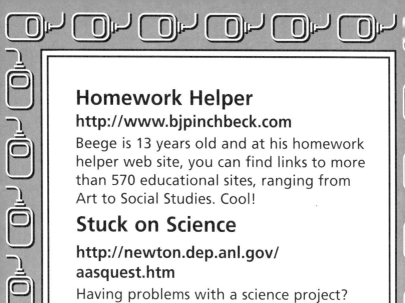

Homework Helper

http://www.bjpinchbeck.com

Beege is 13 years old and at his homework helper web site, you can find links to more than 570 educational sites, ranging from Art to Social Studies. Cool!

Stuck on Science

http://newton.dep.anl.gov/ aasquest.htm

Having problems with a science project? Need an answer in a hurry? Well, here is a site where you can submit a science question, then sit back and await the answer! Easy!

OTHER TITLES IN THE SERIES:

500 of the Weirdest & Wackiest Web Sites
ISBN: 1-902813-29-4

500 of the World's Best Web Sites
ISBN: 1-902813-30-8

500 Indispensable Web Sites for Men
ISBN: 1-902813-67-7